THE NEW NEGRO

Contributors:

Stephen J. Wright

Kenneth B. Clark

Diane Nash

William J. Kenealy, S.J.

Thomas P. Melady

In the symposium:

James Baldwin, Emile Capouya,
Lorraine Hansberry, Nat Hentoff,
Langston Hughes, Alfred Kazin

THE
NEW
NEGRO

Edited by

MATHEW H. AHMANN

FIDES PUBLISHERS • NOTRE DAME, INDIANA

CONTENTS

MATHEW H. AHMANN
*was appointed Executive
Director of the National Catholic
Conference for Interracial Justice at the
time of its formation in 1960. Prior to that
he had been Assistant and then Acting Director of
the Catholic Interracial Council of Chicago. Mr. Ahmann
is a graduate of St. John's University in Collegeville, Minnesota, and has had graduate training in sociology at the
University of Chicago. He is a member of the
National Association for the Advancement of
Colored People, the American Sociological Society, and the National
Catholic Social Action
Conference.*

PREFACE

It is hard, indeed, in the Christian economy of things, to understand how all of us have been able to tolerate monstrous country-wide racial patterns and devices deliberately designed to hold some of our brothers and fellow countrymen in a genuine state of slavery. It is nearly one hundred years since Abraham Lincoln signed the Emancipation Proclamation; the centennial of the signing of this document is January 1, 1963.

But tolerate this racial prejudice and discrimination is precisely what we — and all of the Churches of America — have done for one hundred years. During most of this time the course of race relations has apparently been influenced more by the political balance in our country, and by changes in the economic fortunes of our land, than by the conscience of our Churches, or ourselves. Indeed, the background of the current more speedy and dramatic progress in interracial justice lies in the migration of many of our people during the second World War, and in the fact that a labor shortage in that war created openings in many jobs that before were available only to whites.

Recently we have all seen growing evidence that *people* are consciously seeking a just social order, one free for all our citizens, white and Negro. People increasingly want to shape the social order of the future, as they rightly should. The multiplication since the second World War of public and private organizations and agencies working for interracial justice is one sign. The more dramatic direct-action movements which in the past two years have aroused the conscience of our nation as never before, and have also produced some fast progress in some places in our country, are another. Along with these signs, we have been able to observe a quickening conscience on the racial problem in religion in America, and a greater willingness on the part of our Churches to teach the word of God as they perceive it and to accept an increasing amount of responsibility for leadership in interracial progress.

I think there is a general consciousness in our country that racial prejudice and discrimination are morally wrong. Indeed, among Christians, the charge of heresy is more and more forcefully raised. And racism truly is heresy, for it denies not only the basic equality of all men, but denies also their special relationship in the Redeemer.

There is a general awareness, too, that the racially segregated patterns which run through all forms of life in America are a real impediment to our leadership among the other nations of the world. Racial discrimination and segregation have become a source of great embarrassment to us.

It is only unfortunate that the awareness the average American has of these things, to judge from the general impressions any observer can get from any strata in our society, has not seemed to furnish sufficient motivation for him to face the source of his embarrassment and act more courageously to right the great wrongs that have been perpetuated.

But one thing has changed. Until recently most white Americans had their image of the Negro shaped by prejudiced stereotypes formed and perpetuated by whites. In fact, as Stephen Wright points out in his paper in this book, Negro strategy in fighting for equality accepted and worked within the dominant white image of the Negro. Even the magnificent legal work done by the NAACP did nothing to challenge this image directly.

Now what we call the "New Negro" has changed all this. It is increasingly evident that Negroes will not accept anyone else's definition of themselves. And for the first time, faced with direct and forceful pressure, whites have come face to face with Negroes as they really are. Though this change has been, and is bound to be, unsettling — for it forces us to act — it will produce more and more rapid progress to the free and open society that is the dream of all of us. And this change, this face-to-face confrontation — men face to face with men — is the most significant development in race relations since Lincoln's time.

The National Catholic Conference for Interracial Justice felt it was important to analyze and reflect on these "New Negro" movements, and the confrontation and action which are resulting. We took occasion to do this at our nation-wide convention in Detroit in August, 1961. The papers in this book are the result. Three of these papers — those by Miss Nash, Dr. Wright and Dr. Clark — were given at the convention. The papers by Dr. Melady and William Kenealy, S.J., were prepared to round out the symposium. "The Negro in American Culture," the transcription of an unusual radio broadcast over New York station WBAI-FM, held in early 1961, originally appeared in print in *Cross Currents*. We are indebted to station WBAI-FM, and to the editors of *Cross Currents* for permission to include this transcription in the symposium.

We planned our Detroit convention, and invited people to prepare papers, not merely with our own immediate interests in mind. Rather, we wanted to help make possible some public reflection on the "New Negro" and in inviting these people to contribute, asked them to address themselves to the general American community, not merely to a Catholic audience. We offer these papers, by special arrangement with the publisher, as a contribution to the public understanding of this subject.

A word about the papers.

Stephen Wright's paper on the "New Negro in the South," and Kenneth Clark's on the "New Negro in the North," are analytical pieces which try to explain the rise of current movements, and lay out the probable direction of the future.

Diane Nash is a "Northern" Negro who went to school at Fisk University. Going South for the first time, as she explains, she encountered a pattern of blatant racial discrimination which affected every corner of her life, and the lives of her fellow students. Since experiencing this discrimination, Miss Nash has become one of the leaders of the Nashville Student Movement, and has worked full time for the students on both the sit-ins and the freedom rides. Those who heard her speak in Detroit will say that reading her is no substitute. But I think that her own testimonial to the witness she and her fellow students are giving is a fitting companion-piece to the other papers here.

Father Kenealy's paper takes a different tack from Miss Nash's by forcefully presenting the legal case for the direct-action movements which have sprung up since the first sit-in in Greensboro, North Carolina, in February, 1960.

The ground swell of national movements in Africa has had important overtones for the "New Negro" movements in the United States. Are we willing to tolerate some of the citizens of our country getting their complete freedom after some of the people in Africa? What are the human feelings of an American Negro who sees Africans forging ahead as equals on the world scene, while he is still in bondage in the United States? And, as Thomas Melady points out in his paper, certain situations in Africa are embarrassing to the Catholic Church. If one probed the Portuguese example to its roots, it would probably be as good an illustration as any of the influence of nationalism in taking away the freedom of the Church. In this case, the close relationship in Portugal between the Church and the national policy has indeed limited the vision of the Church.

Finally, we have asked the publisher to add "The Negro in American Culture" to the symposium, because we feel that the candor of its discussion reveals, from the human side, many aspects of the feelings of American Negroes, and of the new movements we are concerned about. Those taking part in the discussion, here transcribed, are sensitive observers and artists and they have something to say to us all.

Mathew H. Ahmann
Executive Director
National Catholic Conference for
Interracial Justice

STEPHEN J. WRIGHT
*is President of Fisk
University of Nashville, Tennessee. Before coming to Fisk in 1957, he
was President of Bluefield State College, and
prior to that, Professor of Education and Dean
of the Faculty at Hampton Institute. Dr. Wright has published widely in professional educational journals, including the*
Journal of Educational Sociology, *the* Journal of Negro
Education, *and the* Harvard Educational Review.
*He is a member of the Board of Directors of
the Southern Regional Council and the
Board of Trustees of the International Institute of Education.*

THE NEW NEGRO
IN THE SOUTH

The South is changing with such rapidity that it is scarcely an exaggeration to refer to what is happening as a revolution — a revolution with many interrelated causes and effects. This section of our nation is becoming rapidly industrialized, rapidly unionized, and rapidly urbanized. These significant changes are having a profound effect upon its politics, its economy, and its racial problems. Cold statistics, however accurate, cannot begin to tell the whole story. Of the changes now in process, the most dramatic are those involving the racial situation — changes which are also destined to have far-reaching effects upon both the economy and the politics of the region. The changes in the racial situation are being attributed, in some quarters, to what is referred to as the "New Negro" in the South.

I shall attempt to present the background from which this "New Negro" emerged, to define and describe him, to suggest some of the principal factors which gave rise to his birth, and to predict something of the impact he will have upon the future development of the region and of the nation.

One cannot understand the New Negro in the South without understanding something of the South itself. "The South," as used hereafter, refers to the eleven states of the old Confederacy: Virginia, North Carolina, South Carolina, Georgia, Florida, Mississippi, Alabama, Arkansas, Louisiana, Tennessee, and Texas. These are the states in which the greater majority of Negroes have lived[1] and which most effectively and systematically enacted their prejudices and their ideas concerning the inferiority of the Negro into law. These are likewise the states which have buttressed their laws with customs which frequently go beyond the law.[2] The combined effect of these laws and customs resulted in a tight, caste-like system of segregation and discrimination which abridged or denied the Negro's right to vote; guaranteed him inferior schools; denied him equal protection under the laws; deprived him of equal employment opportunities; excluded him from public eating places, hotels, places of amusement, and most hospitals; and segregated him on trains, buses, and streetcars. On the other hand, the system did not exclude him from paying taxes or from defending his country in time of war.[3]

For the Negro, it was a system from which there was no escape. Color was the insurmountable wall. Many of the most successful politicians of the region built and sustained their careers on their solemn and vehement promises to maintain the system at *all* costs. The system became a cornerstone of the "southern way of life." The white children were taught its articles of faith and the bitterest reprisals were reserved for those — white or Negro — who sought to change it, or who violated any of its important laws or customs. This, of course, explains why the lynching of Negroes went unpunished; why Negroes who committed crimes against white per-

---

1. Approximately 9,600,000, or 52 per cent of the Negroes in the United States live in these states. In 1950, 60 per cent; in 1930, 71 per cent.

2. Border states such as Maryland, West Virginia and Missouri have had a less comprehensive system of segregation and discrimination and not as rigidly enforced.

3. The term "system," as used here, refers to the total complex of laws, customs and methods of enforcement of segregation and discrimination in the South.

sons received excessive punishment; why congressmen who failed to sign the "Southern Manifesto" placed their political careers in jeopardy; why the white parents who attempted to send their children to desegregated schools in New Orleans were driven out of the city; and why a bus bearing "Freedom Riders" could be burned in Alabama without police interference.

Such a system could be maintained only by force, or by the constant threat of force, and with the consent and support of the great majority of the white people of the region. Until very recent years, even the organized Church gave the system its silent support.

The legal victories in such areas as voting, education, and transportation, and the desegregation of the lunch counters, which have followed in the wake of the student demonstrations, have weakened the system, but its essential philosophy and much of its framework have remained unchanged.

It should be pointed out, however, that there have been, through the years, islands where the system was less rigidly enforced, as well as a few courageous southern whites who have spoken out against aspects of the system, and, in rare instances, against the total system. The number of such persons is very gradually increasing.

One cannot understand the New Negro in the South without understanding the Old Negro in the South, for the New Negro did not spring into existence suddenly; nor did he spring into existence as a totally "New" Negro.

While the Negro in the South has always wanted for himself and his children the same freedom and opportunity which other Americans enjoy, he has not always sought to achieve this by direct, organized pressure. In fact, he has not always been in a position to employ such means, although abortive insurrections for freedom, led by such men as Mark Vesey and Nat Turner, occurred even during the period of slavery.

There were three principal reasons why the Old Negro

in the South could not employ organized pressure to secure his rights and privileges as a citizen:

1.   He was, in the main, a tenant farmer, an unskilled laborer, a domestic servant — incredibly poor and very largely uneducated.

2.   He had nothing approaching responsible police protection. In fact, almost any white person who chose to do so (and many did) could become, without penalty, self-deputized officers to see that he stayed in "his place." As Cash has pointed out, the southern Negro became almost open game when the courts were returned to southern hands following the Reconstruction:

> In many districts, particularly in the deep South, the killing of a Negro by a white man ceased, in practice, even to call for legal inquiry. But wherever and whenever the forms were observed, the coroner or the jury was all but sure to call it "self defense," or "justifiable homicide" and to free the slayer with celerity. And if any black was fantastic enough to run to the court house with redress for a beating or any other wrong, he stood a good chance (provided he was heard at all) not only of seeing his assailant go scot-free, but of finding the onus somehow shifted to himself, or of finding himself in the dock on some other count, and of ending by going to a chain gang at the mercies of persons hand-picked for their skill in adjusting his sense of reality.[4]

3.   He had few leaders who commanded his or anyone else's respect. From about 1896, when he made his famous Atlanta Exposition Speech, until his death in 1915, Booker T. Washington was, without doubt, the most powerful single Negro leader the South had known. During the period when the southern Negro was being systematically disenfranchised, Washington advocated, with almost irresistible eloquence, that the Negro devote his efforts and his energies to educating and improving

---

4. W. J. Cash, *The Mind of the South*, (New York: Knopf, 1941).

himself, and urged him to trust the southern white man to grant him his civil rights when he deserved them. "The great thing," counseled Washington, "is to conduct ourselves so as to become worthy of the privileges of an American citizen, and these privileges will come." Many Negroes came to believe Washington's teachings.

Thus deprived of the vote, largely uneducated, having very few militant and informed leaders (W. E. B. Du Bois was one of the conspicuous exceptions), and denied equal protection under the law, the Negro in the South, in the main, developed survival accommodations and participated in what Doyle has called the "etiquette of race relations in the South" — i.e., a code of behavior consistent with the caste-like restrictions which the customs and laws of the region imposed upon him.[5] He tended to put his faith in good race relations, which meant not disturbing the status quo to the point of reprisals, and such gains as he achieved were made by saying what the white southerner wanted to hear and by frequently acting the role the white southerner wanted to see. In so doing, the Old Negro in the South helped to perpetuate the stereotype or image in which the white South wanted to believe and which it needed in order to justify the laws and customs which constituted its system of segregation and discrimination.

This, then, is the Negro the white South "understands." The fact is, he no longer exists. In reality, he never existed.

Both the "etiquette" and the strategies employed by the southern Negro changed as the "logistics" of the situation changed. Following World War I, the Negro newspapers, as organs of protest, gained stature; the *Crisis,* the organ of the NAACP under the dynamic editorship of Du Bois, stepped up its crusade against lynchings; the NAACP, as an organization, became strong enough to begin what was to become a systematic and

---

5. See: Bertram W. Doyle, *The Etiquette of Race Relations in the South* (Chicago: University of Chicago Press, 1937).

highly successful attack on both the legal foundations of the southern system and the more flagrant reprisals used against Negroes to sustain the system; the separate but "equal" educational system improved; the decay of southern tenancy progressed more rapidly than was evident to anyone except the scholars; thousands of Negroes migrated to the North; Booker T. Washington's counsel was being repudiated by the new leaders; the economic position of the Negro improved slowly but surely; a young lawyer, Thurgood Marshall, forced the University of Maryland, in 1935, to admit a Negro, Donald Murray, to its law school; the *principle* of equal salaries for Negro teachers was established by the federal courts; the Supreme Court ruled that the state of Missouri had only the alternative of admitting Lloyd Gaines, a Negro, to its law school at the University of Missouri, or of providing an equal one for him *within* the state; and "graduate" schools for Negroes in the state-supported colleges in the South mushroomed following the Gaines decision. The development of these "graduate" schools was designed to prevent Negroes from applying for admission to the white schools of the South.

World War II came, with its unprecedented demand for manpower, and before peace was declared, Negroes had been admitted to all branches of the armed services, and Executive Order 8802, laying the basis for FEPC legislation, had been signed.

The foregoing developments had been made possible largely by Negro protests, and by their legal and political action. In the process, the Negro had gained new friends and new allies. He had also learned, in the process, that almost no one could help him if he did not press for his own cause, but that many could and would help him fight for his rights as a citizen.

By the end of World War II, the southern Negro was not a "New Negro," but he was significantly different from the Negro who was disenfranchised following the Reconstruction; he was different from the Negro who began, following World War I, to learn that the world had not been "made safe for democracy"; he was also different from the Negro who put his faith in good race relations in the belief that, as he became a competent citizen, the rights and privileges of citizenship would be *conferred* upon him. Also by the end of World War II, more than a million tenant farmers, with their dependence upon white landlords, had left the farms.

Contrary to popular opinion, the New Negro in the South was not born with the student demonstrations in 1960. If an actual date could be set, the evidence would tend to place it about 1945, and certainly between 1945 and 1950.

One of the things which gave rise to the New Negro in the South was the slowness and resistance with which the southern white responded to the Negro's representations for first-class citizenship. This slowness and resistance made the Negro impatient. For example, it took four years and a great deal of money to have the Supreme Court declare illegal the white primary which excluded Negroes from voting. It took three more years to have the same court strike down the cynical device adopted by Texas and seven other states to confer upon the Executive Committee of the Democratic Committees in the South what amounted to the right to exclude Negroes from voting. Moreover, it took approximately four years from the time that the first desegregation case was filed in Clarendon County, South Carolina, to secure a ruling of the Supreme Court in 1954 which outlawed segregation in the public schools. Finally, the slowness of the "all deliberate speed" with which the decision was carried out merely added to the Negro's impatience.

During the war, the nation had experienced a revival of idealism, a new concern for the extension of the great blessings and promises of democracy to all. A war fought to preserve the Four Freedoms could not, in fairness, exclude Negroes. It was a climate of opinion in which

Negro protests could be heard. In the North, some conspicuous gains in employment and housing had been made. Discrimination in most hotels and many places of amusement was disappearing. The southern Negro was aware of these gains.

The South, on the other hand, sought with its usual resourcefulness to maintain its "way of life." The educational system for Negroes continued to be unequal; voting rights in the deep South continued to be abridged or denied; exclusion from the overwhelming majority of the white-collar jobs continued as a studied policy, the major exception being teaching in Negro schools; and segregation in transportation was substantially unchanged. In other words, the system was substantially what it was in 1930, or even earlier. In some states like Mississippi and Alabama, it was substantially what it was in 1900! But the Negro of the South was different. By this time, he had learned three bitter lessons:

1. That the white South would never voluntarily dismantle the Jim Crow system. On the contrary, it would at all costs, through legislation, legal circumventions, and reprisals, where necessary, seek to preserve it.

2. That no substantial changes in his status and relationships would ever result from good race relations as they were conceived in the South, and that the time would never come when he would, in the mind of the white South, be "ready" to have the rights and privileges of full citizenship conferred upon him.

3. That the only effective way to change his status was to employ with vigor and imagination the instruments of pressure: the courts, the vote, his economic power, and protests of a variety of types and, further, that any leader who counselled otherwise had outlived his usefulness.

In other words, the system of Jim Crow had come to be understood for what it was, and with that knowledge it was realized that new and more effective means were now needed to achieve the long-denied, cherished ends of full citizenship. When these lessons were learned, the "New Negro" of the South was born.

The new approaches, the new means to old ends were heard from platforms all over the South from a wide variety of leaders, and they were read in Negro newspapers, in books and in articles written by Negroes. The disparities which existed between the Negro's situation and the opportunities to which he, in a democracy, was entitled, were set forth with irrefutable accuracy.[6] Even the ends were more clearly stated. Dr. Harry V. Richardson, then President of Gammon Theological Seminary, speaking before a Negro organization in Atlanta, stated them as clearly as any one:

> He [the Negro] wants that every Southern child shall be able to live and grow and learn in the South, without having the stigma of inferiority stamped on his skin or burned into his soul.
>
> He wants the right to secure any kind of work of which he is capable, without being denied because of his skin.
>
> He wants access to every public privilege or service to which as a citizen he is entitled, without having to crawl in through the back doors or stand behind screens like an outcast or a dog.
>
> He wants an American's participation in the processes of his government, receiving all rights and bearing all responsibilities.
>
> This is what he wants, this is all he wants and he believes under God this is fair.

---

6. See such works as: J. Saunders Redding, *On Being Negro* (Indianapolis: Bobbs-Merrill, 1951); Carl Rowan, *South of Freedom* (New York: Knopf, 1952), *Go South to Sorrow* (New York: Random House, 1957); Walter White, *How Far the Promised Land?* (New York: Viking Press, 1956); Richard Wright, *White Man, Listen!* (New York: Doubleday, 1957), *Color Curtain* (New York: World Publishing Co., 1956); Pauli Murray, *State Laws on Race and Color;* and the yearbook issues of the *Journal of Negro Education.*

Not only does the New Negro want these things. He wants them now!

As the New Negro began to apply his new means, the effects began to be felt. In the eleven states of the Old Confederacy, voting registrations increased from 595,000 in 1947 to more than 1,238,000 in 1956. By 1960, they had increased another 28,000.[7] In brief, the number of registrants more than doubled. More significant than the increase, in a sense, was the fact that the increase was achieved over intimidations which included violence, threats, and economic reprisals, as well as involved discriminatory tactics. The effect of the increase in voting could be seen in the election of Negroes to city councils in places like Richmond, Greensboro, and Nashville, and in the election of Dr. Rufus E. Clement, President of Atlanta University, to the Atlanta Board of Education, although in the latter case, votes other than those of Negroes played a significant role. The increased use of the ballot has had two discernible effects:

1. In states where the largest numbers of Negroes vote, the arch segregationist candidates for public office are having a difficult time winning elections, and this is encouraging the more moderate politicians to speak out with more courage with respect to Negro rights. The recent federal elections in Tennessee are cases in point.

2. The success with the ballot is doubtless encouraging even more Negroes to vote.

But it has been in the struggle for equal educational opportunity that the application of new means and new methods has been more spectacular. The new means began with a rash of cases filed in federal district courts for equal facilities. The NAACP received more requests for legal assistance than it could provide. Furthermore, each city, each county or district was a separate case. Unfortunately, the cases were being handled within the framework of the separate but equal doctrine. In 1950,

---

7. Margaret Price, *The Negro Voter in the South* (Atlanta: The Southern Regional Council, 1956).

however, the NAACP wisely decided to deal with the fundamental issue: the legality of segregation in the public school, the real cause of the inequality. Clarendon County in South Carolina in 1951 became the first such case to be filed. The system was under attack and reprisals began almost immediately. Bank mortgages on the homes and farms of the participants were called; shotguns were fired into Negro homes; Negro homes were set fire in the dead of the night. But not a single Negro parent withdrew his child from the list of plaintiffs. This is an example of the New Negro which can be multiplied many times in a number of different situations where the instruments of pressure — the vote, the courts, the boycott, the protest — are being used, in the face of reprisals, to attack the system.

What is the New Negro like? Is he only the educated Negro? How does he differ from the Negro prior to 1945? A few examples will help to provide answers to these questions. Many white southerners pretend to believe that the new militancy of Negroes is caused by northern or outside agitators. This is nonsense. The incident involving Spottswood W. Robinson, III, now Dean of the Law School at Howard University and a member of the Civil Rights Commission, but at that time (1951) an NAACP lawyer practicing in Richmond, Virginia, suggests the truth:

> Robinson went with some trepidation to a meeting of Prince Edward County Negro parents to tell them, as he put it, that the NAACP had decided to "hit segregation head on and no longer fool around with the separate-but-equal business. . . . I took great pains, and I will readily confess that perhaps I belabored the question in pointing out why we felt this was necessary. I told them that if they were not ready to make the decision immediately, they could go home and think it over and then come to another meeting to decide."
>
> A father in the rear of the church rose to ask, "I have one question. As I understand the position of the

NAACP, it is impossible for our children to get equality so long as we have segregation. Is that correct?"

"Yes, sir," answered Robinson.

The parent looked quietly at Robinson and told him, "Well, we have known that in this county for a long time, and we have been simply waiting for you and the NAACP to find out the same thing."[8]

The Montgomery bus boycott grew out of an incident involving the refusal of Mrs. Rosa Parks, a seamstress, to relinquish her bus seat to a white passenger. Her action was not suggested by any "outsider" or northern "agitator."

This boycott illustrates several characteristics of the New Negro. For more than a year, the old and the young, the educated and the uneducated, boycotted the buses. When other transportation was not available, they walked. The boycott could not have been successful without discipline, cooperation, and sacrifice on the part of many. One of the most poignant and illustrative stories to come out of the Montgomery bus boycott involved an elderly Negro woman trudging along with obvious difficulty. One of the pool drivers stopped beside her and said, "Jump in, grandmother. You don't need to walk." She waved him on. "I'm not walking for myself," she explained. "I'm walking for my children and my grandchildren."[9]

The Montgomery bus boycott was an attack upon the southern system and, in conformity with the pattern, it drew reprisals, including the bombing of the home of Martin Luther King, Jr., the leader of the movement. Again, the reprisals were met with fortitude and courage by leaders and followers alike.

Few instances of courage and poise exceed that exhibited by the Negro children who attended the Cen-

---

8. As quoted in Walter White, *How Far the Promised Land?*, p. 47.

9. Martin Luther King, Jr., *Stride Toward Freedom* (New York: Harper, 1958), p. 61.

tral High School in Little Rock in the face of daily heck-
ling and threatened mob violence which finally required
the use of army troops.

The Tuskegee boycott grew out of the effort of the
state of Alabama to gerrymander Negroes out of the
town of Tuskegee, fearing their potential voting strength.
Many of the Negroes involved were the educated members of the staff of Tuskegee and the nearby veteran's
hospital. In addition to boycotting the Tuskegee merchants, they fought the state of Alabama through to the
Supreme Court of the United States and won a clear-cut
victory. This case illustrates the disciplined and skillful
use of two instruments of pressure — the economic and
the legal.[10]

The enormous increase in NAACP membership in
the South is another example of aroused concern.

The foregoing examples illustrate the character of
the New Negro of the South:

1. He represents no particular class;
2. He is confident that he can, by the use of the instruments of pressure, improve his status;
3. He is willing to make serious sacrifices in order
to do so;
4. He is, for the most part, led by intelligent and
courageous individuals, vastly different from the "Uncle
Toms" of former years, prominent among them being
the educated young minister and especially the lawyer.[11]

In the late winter of 1960, the "sit-in" demonstrations
exploded in a climate of opinion which was ripe and
which almost guaranteed their success from the outset.
Since these demonstrations have perhaps been the best
reported effort in the Negro's long struggle for equality,

10. For an interesting account of the setting of the Tuskegee
boycott and the legal aspects of the gerrymander case, see the
articles entitled: "Gomillion versus Lightfoot," in the June 10
and 17, 1961, issues of *The New Yorker*.

11. Thurgood Marshall is so popular among Negroes that Arna
Bontemps has labeled him a "folk-hero." See Arna Bontemps,
100 Years of Negro Freedom (New York: Dodd, Mead, 1961).

I shall not attempt to review in any detail what has happened, but rather to analyze what has happened.

Whether the demonstration is a lunch counter "sit-in," a theatre line "stand-in," a pool "wade-in," or a "Freedom Rider," the activity involves essentially one or more students exercising some right or privilege which he, in the South, is denied either by law or by custom solely because of his race. This means that the demonstration is a direct attack on the southern Jim Crow system, and since it is, the student is exposed immediately to the standard southern method of dealing with such violators — the reprisal. The fact that the violator is a neat, courteous, non-violent college student makes little or no difference to those who are responsible for law and order.[12]

Shortly after the demonstrations began, those responsible for law and order made three serious mistakes:

1.   They arrested the students, in mass, under a variety of charges: loitering, trespassing, disturbing the peace, conspiracy to obstruct trade and commerce, etc. (Most of these charges would not stand up in a fair court of record.[13])

2.   They allowed the white hoodlums to beat up or otherwise molest the demonstrators without, in most cases, even the penalty of arrest.

3.   The governors, or in some instances, state boards of education, expelled or threatened to expel participating students who were enrolled in state colleges.[14]

---

12. It should be understood that the New Negro of the South also includes small groups who would achieve their ends by more drastic techniques.   Examples would include the Black Muslims. (See Eric Lincoln's *Black Muslims* (Boston: Beacon Press, 1961) and Julian Mayfield's "Challenge to Negro Leadership," *Commentary*, April, 1961.)

13. These cases have, in the main, been handled in police courts.

14. To date some forty Negro students have been expelled from state-supported institutions for Negroes for participation in student demonstrations.

The immediate effect of these actions was that of cementing the Negro adult community in support of the students — adults from all classes. In Nashville, for example, the cementing of the adult community was expressed in a number of ways:

1. The ten Negro lawyers in the city contributed their services in defending the students;
2. In one afternoon, bond in the amount of $40,000 was posted;
3. A boycott of downtown stores which lasted for more than a month and was almost 100 per cent effective was conducted.

This latter activity, as in the majority of instances, was decisive in the opening of the lunch counters.

Conducting the demonstrations with a courageous, non-violent approach, usually with a willingness to serve jail sentences, the students have not only frustrated those responsible for "law and order," but they have, in my judgment, achieved the following results:

1. Advertised to the nation and indeed to the world the ridiculousness of the southern Jim Crow System and have helped to create a climate and a sentiment essential to the solution of this deep-seated problem.
2. Provided the nation and especially the South with a much more accurate image of the southern Negro, and particularly the young southern Negro.
3. Provided themselves with leadership training of immeasurable value — training which no institution could provide.
4. Demonstrated that direct pressure can be a powerful factor in accelerating changes in the racial situation in the South.
5. Opened, with the help of the Negro adult community and liberal whites, lunch counters in some twenty-eight southern cities and counties.
6. Aroused the southern conscience on racial issues especially where the organized Church is concerned.
7. Inspired many of their tired and disillusioned

elders to rededicate themselves to the cause with new vigor.

It should be made clear, however, that student demonstrations cannot be a panacea for the racial ills of the South. They can never be an adequate substitute for responsible adult civic participation and action: intelligent voting, the use of the courts, the intelligent use of economic power, and the giving of effect to the new gains. It should also be pointed out that as impressive as the student demonstrators' achievements are, the power structure of the South is still very much intact and, until it is changed or its attitudes radically modified, the major problems of voting, equal employment opportunity, equal access to housing, the schools, hospitals, and hotels will remain in the realm of unsolved problems.

Nothing that I have said, however, alters the fact that the student demonstrators are a significant and dynamic part of the New Negro in the South. They are near the voting age and are destined to become a part of a great reservoir of intelligent and courageous leadership, sensitive and dedicated to problems confronting Negroes in the South. In the long run, this latter point may become even more important than their achievements to date.

The Negro student demonstrations also focused attention on the Negro college student generally and on the role that education is playing in developing the New Negro in the South. Negro institutions of higher learning in the region enroll more than seventy thousand students, and their education includes an understanding of America "as a civilization" and a way of life as well as their duties and responsibilities as citizens. When twenty-seven students of Fisk University were arrested in February of 1960 for engaging in sit-in demonstrations, as President of the University, I issued the following statement to the press which reflects something of the spirit of the Negro college of the South, especially the *private* college:

As President of the University, I approve the ends our students are seeking by these demonstrations. From all I have been able to learn, they have broken no law by the means they have employed thus far, and they have not only conducted themselves peaceably, but with poise and dignity. As long as this is true, I have no present intention of instructing them to discontinue their efforts. The point at issue, it seems to me, is not how to stop their efforts but rather to find better alternative ways to end segregation in the public eating places of the city . . . .

I would hope sincerely that the constructive citizens of our community would seek ways by which this can be accomplished. After all, these are fine young citizens who, in their post-college years, will make significant contributions to the nation. Moreover, they have been exposed, all their lives, to the teachings of the great American scriptures of democracy, freedom and equality, and no literate person should be surprised that they reflect these teachings in their conduct. In the meantime, it is my hope that they will receive the sympathetic understanding of our community and the responsible protection of the police.

In other words, the education Negroes have received is doing for the Negro what education of the right type has always done for people, i.e., it has given them a sense and an appreciation for freedom.

The New Negro in the South, with his new instruments of pressure, his increasing self-confidence, and a new leadership which is *earning* the right to lead, will inevitably make significant changes in his status, despite the stiffening resistance of the white South. In assuming his new posture, he has placed himself in position to be helped a great deal more by both the "moderate" and the liberal white southerners, as well as by many others who understand the national and international significance of the stakes involved in the struggle.

In addition to the official white South which enforces the laws and customs of the region, there are many con-

cerned white southerners who labor against heavy odds
to hasten the day when equality of opportunity will be
accorded all citizens of the region. Many of these individuals are members and supporters of the Southern
Regional Council and its state and local affiliates. The
Council, which is thoroughly interracial, is one of the
most constructive and effective organizations working
in the field of race relations. Its monthly periodical,
New South, together with its special studies and releases
constitute what is, in my opinion, the most accurate and
extensive current information on racial problems in the
South. Examples of its studies include *The Negro Voter
in the South,* one of the best sources of information on
the subject, and their excellent and widely quoted report
prepared for President Kennedy entitled *The Federal
Executive and Civil Rights.* The report states (and docu-
ments) that the President holds power under the Constitution and existing statutes which, if used, "could
carry the country far toward good race relations." The
influence of the Council and its affiliates is enormous.

The majority of the white Churches in the South
have now, through their denominational organizations,
condemned segregation and discrimination. A number
of city ministerial associations have done likewise. Unfortunately, however, examples of positive action by
local churches are very difficult to find.

In addition to the leavening that will come from
within the South, the fact that the peoples of the underdeveloped nations of Asia, Africa, and South America
are gaining their freedom and self-respect has already
begun to have its reverberations in the South.

The Communists' exploitation of the American racial
paradox will also have its effect. The federal government's new emphasis on civil rights, with the new laws
of 1957 and 1960, will undoubtedly increase the New
Negro's use of the ballot. Likewise, the federal government's interest in seeing that the Negro has a fair
chance to secure equal employment opportunities where

government contracts are involved will improve his economic status.

The education of the Negro in the South will improve beyond any question, and no one can predict the magnitude of the long-run effect of this education.

If the foregoing factors and forces run their expected courses, we can, I think, predict the following with reasonable certainty:

1. That with the coming of the unlimited right to vote, the New Negro in the South will help to retire from public service the racial demagogues who build their political careers on the exploitation of the racial situation and who, in the process, sow seeds of hate which may some day reap a bitter harvest;

2. That with better economic and educational opportunities, the New Negro in the South will do much to help raise the economic level of the South. The system has forced large numbers of Negroes to be a part of the problem of poverty in the South, rather than a part of the answer to its eradication. The long relief rolls and much of the petty crime which characterize the Negro ghettos are direct products of the system;

3. That the nation will be the beneficiary of the talents and genius of many thousands of young Negroes who, under the system, either fail to be developed or atrophy. This is a luxury which this nation in these demanding times cannot afford.

The speed with which these predictions will occur will depend upon a number of factors which no one can accurately assess, the principal ones being:

1. *The role the federal government will play.* The government has, in the cases of Little Rock and Montgomery, interfered with the South's use of the violent reprisal. If it continues to do so, the New Negro will be able to continue to exercise the processes of democracy to improve his status.

2. *The attitude of northern business operating in the South.* Southern business is almost inextricably inter-

woven with Northern business. In 1957, for example, *The Nation* pointed out that National Cash Register had 150 sales and service outlets in the South with some 2,300 salesmen; that the Prudential Life Insurance Company had 245 southern sales offices with approximately 5,000 employees.[15] In addition, chain stores like Woolworth, Sears Roebuck, and many others have branches or outlets in the region. *The New Republic* calls attention to the situation in Birmingham:

> More than any other city in the South, Birmingham is dominated by Northern capital. It is not a Southern city at all in terms of control or culture. It is the city of U. S. Steel, of those who play the game Steel's way, and good race relations have never been an apparent concern to steel. Backing from Steel and the financial powers of Birmingham for (Bull) Conner, for the brilliant racist and former governor, Frank M. Dixon, and for former Congressman Laurie Battle (who played on prejudice in his 1959 effort against Senator John Sparkman with evangelical fervor) has kept race a throbbing issue. . . .
>
> What about the Birmingham Press? The morning *Post-Herald* has long been a member of the Scripps-Howard chain, based in the North, and the afternoon *News* was sold by local owners not long ago to Newhouse, another Yankee chain publisher. What is the stand of these Northern-owned newspapers on segregation? It could not be more faithful to Southern segregation tradition.
>
> Who's to blame for the shame of Birmingham? The people who live there, and the elected officials, local and state, who wink, and the law, of course. *But behind them run lines of economic and political power straight into New York, Washington and other cities.* [Emphasis supplied.] The belief is inescapable that if the men at the other ends of these lines were to act with courage

---

15. *The Nation*, October 12, 1957, p. 234.

and in terms of the highest moral and national interest,
they could improve things in Birmingham.[16]

The problem extends far beyond Birmingham. The
reported discrimination against Negroes in the Lockheed
plant at Marietta, Georgia, with a million-dollar government contract, is but another example.

3. *National public opinion.* There are those who
hold, and many are in the North, that the Negro should
not push the issue, that he faces the danger of alienating
his "friends" or potential "friends." The Negro and those
who understand the issues at stake must inform the
larger public that if the issue is not pushed, nothing
happens except a continuation of the system; that unless
the "time" for which the white southerners plead so
eloquently is actually *used* by them to make constructive
changes, it has no healing virtue. As Gordon W. Allport
points out: "The world is too small, too crowded, too
perilous, and too rapidly changing to permit further
temporizing with bigotry and discrimination!"[17]

4. *The emergence of a new southern leadership.*
There are leaders in the South who recognize the incom-
putable damage the system does to white and Negroes
alike, as well as to the nation in the eyes of the rest of
the world. They recognize also the ultimate futility of
the effort to defend it and the hypocrisy which its defense involves. The question is, when will a new crop
of political and business leaders begin to make these facts
their platform?

Take any group of human beings and provide them
with inferior education; deny them the right to vote;
deny them equal job opportunities; force them to live in
ghettos; and exclude them from hotels, public eating
places, and even hospitals, and, developed under such

---

16. Quoted in *New South*, July-August, 1960, p. 8.
17. Quoted in *The Christian Century*, May 24, 1961.

conditions, they will scarcely be able to compete as first-class citizens, unless they are supermen.

The Negro of the South has lived under these conditions for nearly one hundred years and he is seeking, in constructive ways, to change them. One cannot be exposed to the great American dream and not seek to become a part of that dream. In seeking to become a part of that dream, the Negro of the South helps to make that dream come true, not only for himself, but for the South and for the nation, and he deserves the help of both.

KENNETH B. CLARK

*is Professor of
Psychology at the College of
the City of New York and Research
Director of the Northside Center for
Child Development. He has written extensively
on race relations and desegregation, and his study
of the effects of prejudice and discrimination on the
personality development of children was cited by the Supreme
Court in its 1954 decision banning segregation in public
education. Since 1951 Dr. Clark has been Social
Science Consultant to the legal and educational staff of the NAACP and in 1961
was awarded the NAACP's annual
Spingarn Medal for distinguished achievement by
an American Negro.*

THE NEW NEGRO
IN THE NORTH

The New Negro in the North cannot be understood in isolation. He must be understood in terms of the early and, particularly, the recent history of the Negro in the United States and the complexity and interrelatedness of the pattern of civil rights, political, economic, and international developments characteristic of our times.

In the nineteenth century the Negro population in America was largely concentrated in the South. Around World War I the Negro population began a major migration from southern to northern areas. This migration of Negroes from southern rural areas to northern urban centers continued at a steady pace from World War I through World War II and has continued during the past two decades. At the present there are nearly twenty million Negroes in America and 55 per cent of them live in cities. Fourteen metropolitan areas throughout the country have Negro communities of from two hundred thousand to more than a million people. In the New York metropolitan area there are over a million and a half Negroes; a million Negroes reside in the Chicago area; and one out of every four residents in Philadelphia is a Negro. Washington, D. C., has the distinction of being the only major metropolitan area in the country in which the majority — 53 per cent — of the residents are Negroes.

The increasing concentration of the American Negro

population in such northern urban communities as New York, Chicago, Philadelphia, Detroit, Cleveland, Los Angeles, Baltimore, and Washington, D. C., presents some obvious and significant political implications. Negroes who are free to vote in these communities — with the exception of Washington, D. C., where everyone is disenfranchised — have the balance of political power in these states which have a large concentration of electoral votes. If and when Negroes are required to vote in terms of critical racial issues, they could and do exert tremendous political power, particularly in presidential elections. It is significant also that there are at present Negro congressmen from New York City, Chicago, Detroit, and Philadelphia and it is reasonable to expect that within the near future there will be additional demonstrations of increased political power of Negroes in these communities. As the Negro increases his political power in northern communities he will influence the status of Negroes in the southern states and facilitate the general progress toward full social, political, and economic equality.

The shift in the Negro population from the late nineteenth century pattern of southern rural to a mid-twentieth century pattern of northern urban must be understood in terms of the more basic shift of our economy from an agrarian one to its present highly industrialized form. The use of Negro labor in the factories in the North has resulted in significant increases in the economic status of the Negro. The average income of Negro families in the North is approximately $4,000 annually while the average income of Negro families in the South is a little more than $3,000 annually. This general increase in economic status of Negroes provides the basis for the accelerated increase in the number of Negroes who can move into the middle class and compete for the middle-class success symbols of home, education for their children, clothing, and various necessities and luxuries.

Another fact in the recent history of the Negro which must be taken into account in understanding the present status of the Negro in America is the general social and economic advances which occurred during the Roosevelt New Deal era. Although civil rights issues were not as clearly focussed in the 1930's as they are now, the effect of the New Deal in stabilizing the general economy benefited Negroes as well as other economically disadvantaged groups. Probably the most dramatic civil rights development during the Roosevelt era was the ability of A. Philip Randolph to extract from President Franklin Roosevelt the executive order setting up the Fair Employment Practices Committee in the federal government. It may be of some historical significance that this first FEPC came from a liberal, progressive administration only as a consequence of a threat of a mass march on Washington by Negroes. It is also significant to note that the March on Washington movement was largely a northern Negro movement.

With the advent of World War II the Negro's pressure on the federal government for relief from the more flagrant forms of racial stigma and segregation increased. The demands for desegregation of the armed services were intensified and met with some success during the Truman administration. Significant civil rights litigation instigated by the legal staff of the NAACP in the late 1930's was increased in extent, depth, and tempo and culminated in the historic Brown decision of May 17, 1954. This decision overruled the Plessy "separate but equal" doctrine which had dominated judicial decisions in civil rights litigation from 1896. It established the new judicial precedent that all laws which required or permitted racial segregation in public education violated the equal protection clause of the Fourteenth Amendment of the United States Constitution. Subsequent decisions of the United States Supreme Court clearly indicated that the essence of the Brown decision is applicable to problems of state-imposed segregation in other areas of American life such as transportation and state-supported public recreational facilities. While these civil rights cases involved Negro plaintiffs from southern or border states, they were made possible through the combined efforts of the NAACP lawyers and expert witnesses who were from the North as well as from the South. During the trial and appellate phases of these cases there was a necessary and close partnership of northern and southern Negroes as well as some whites.

The increasing success of the Negro in his fight against discrimination in the various areas of American life reflects not only the increased political and economic power of Negroes in the North and the increasing power of Negroes in the South but also reflects the heightened morale and determination of the Negro. Probably the most important single factor contributing to this increased determination and morale among Negroes is the May 17, 1954, decision of the Supreme Court. It is difficult to overestimate the value of this decision in understanding the present psychology of the Negro in the North and in the South. The dramatic impact of this decision — the simple, eloquent language of color-blind justice which its words convey — in effect reassured the Negro that his belief in equality and the justice of his cause was not pious wishful thinking. His beliefs and hopes were now reaffirmed by the United States Supreme Court, the most important judicial branch of the federal government. The Brown decision confirmed the Negro's faith in the basic validity and resilience of American democracy. At the same time, it stimulated him to intensify his attacks against all vestiges of racial segregation and discrimination which remained in American life.

The Montgomery bus boycotts; the sit-in movements conducted with restraint and efficiency by Negro college students; the "freedom rides" which Negro and white students, adults, and members of the clergy have used so effectively to dramatize the continued violation of the rights of Negro citizens in interstate transportation; and the increased concern of many northern communities with the problems of de facto segregation in public schools are some examples of the heightened morale and irresistible determination of the Negro population to free our nation from the shackles of racial segregation.

In spite of the interrelatedness of civil rights activities in the North and in the South, there are some significant regional differences in the nature of the specific problems and the general pattern of the civil rights struggle. The most obvious difference is the fact that many southern states still attempt to maintain patterns of segregation and discrimination through laws and the use of the power of the police and political authorities in spite of the recent clear decisions of the United States Supreme Court. Northern patterns of segregation and discrimination, however, exist in spite of laws against them and in spite of protestations of elected political officials. Northern patterns of segregation and discrimination reflect among other things custom, habit, apathy, conflicts and inconsistencies among whites and some Negroes.

Another crucial difference is the fact that the Negro in the northern states has been able to register and to vote and thereby exert the necessary political power to obtain state laws against discrimination in employment, housing, education, and public accommodations. Systematic interference or discouragement of the Negro's right to vote in southern states has successfully kept him politically impotent. He therefore has been unable to influence politicians and the other governmental officials who pass the laws and make decisions which are frequently in conflict with the desires and interests of the masses of Negroes in these states. It would seem that as long as the average elected official in the South continues to see the electorate only in terms of whites he will continue to seek election and re-election in terms of the lowest common denominator of racist appeals.

In effect, he too will remain a captive of the racists.
The present drive to increase the number of Negroes
who are registered voters in southern states is a significant development toward the goal of increasing the
political power of southern Negroes and a necessary step
toward major civil rights progress in America.

The Negro in the North is no longer plagued by
flagrant signs or examples of racial segregation in public
transportation, recreation, theaters, movies, and higher
education. For the northern Negro racism takes more
subtle forms. The pattern of discrimination against the
Negro in northern communities tends generally to be
inconsistent and capricious, particularly in areas of
public accommodation. The most persistent vestiges of
systematic discrimination against Negroes in northern
communities are found in the areas of residential
segregation — ghetto housing — and de facto segregation
in the schools. It is frequently stated that de facto
segregated schools in the North reflect primarily the
basic patterns of residential segregation and can be
cured only when more democratic housing patterns
are achieved in northern urban communities. Some
observers, however, have suggested the possibility that
the relationship between de facto segregated schools
and patterns of residential segregation is more cyclic
than the more usual and simple cause-and-effect interpretation would suggest. Segregated housing causing
segregated schools may be no more valid an interpretation than the possibility that de facto segregated
schools, brought about through gerrymandering, could
facilitate the process of residential segregation.

In spite of the fact that a number of northern states
such as New York, Massachusetts, and Michigan have
fairly strong laws against racial discrimination in employment, there is rather consistent evidence that this
type of discrimination nevertheless persists in these
states. The progress in this sphere cannot mask the
pervasive residual patterns of racial discrimination in

employment. The role of labor unions in the perpetuation of these violations must be examined with more tough-minded realism.

The northern Negro's techniques and methods must not only be appropriate to the specific and more subtle type of civil rights problems found in the North but must also contribute to the solution of the larger national civil rights struggle. Furthermore, the inter-relatedness of the increased tempo of civil rights activities among Negroes throughout America and the rapid progress of African states from colonialism to the dignity of independent nations, spurs specific and intensified desegregation activities among Negroes in northern communities. Examples of such concentrated desegregation activities may be found in the program for the desegregation of the de facto segregated schools in New York City; the unprecedented litigation before the federal courts for the desegregation of a de facto segregated school in New Rochelle, New York; the attempt on the part of Negroes in Chicago to break the pattern of racial segregation on the beaches of their city; and the effective program of selective buying organized by a group of Negro ministers in Philadelphia.

The metropolitan press, national magazines, radio, and television have given considerable attention to the activities, ideology, and demonstrations of black nationalist groups. These black nationalists, who have been accurately described as the contemporary descendants of the Garvey movement of the 1920's, are, like the Garvey movement, predominantly, if not exclusively, a northern urban social phenomenon. Probably the most influential of these groups are the Black Muslims, whose national leadership and headquarters are located in Chicago. The strength of the rapidly growing Black Muslims appears to be concentrated in Chicago, New York, Boston, Detroit, and Philadelphia. Recently there seems to be some evidence that the movement has gotten a fairly strong foothold in one southern city, Atlanta,

Georgia. The philosophy of the Black Muslims and the
other black nationalist groups is rather simple and direct.
It is a philosophy of hatred and despair reflecting the
American racist simplification of the importance of skin
color. The dramatic twist which these groups give to
American racism is that they preach the supremacy of
blacks and the inherent degradation of whites. This
reversal is dramatic, disturbing, and terrifying to whites
and to some middle- and upper-class Negroes.

The Black Muslims and most, if not all, of the other
nationalistic groups appeal to the more marginal Negro.
They recruit most successfully from the lower socio-
economic classes, and a high proportion of their members have been in conflict with the law. As C. Eric
Lincoln has pointed out in his book *The Black Muslims
in America,* this group does a most effective job in
rehabilitating members. It is ironic that these essentially
cultist groups are markedly more effective in raising
the morale of their members, giving some purpose and
meaning to their lives, than are the more acceptable
social institutions and the traditional Churches. The
explanation for this irony may be found in the basic
truth in the argument of the leaders of this group:
namely, that our middle-class society in inflicting or
accepting the stigma and humiliation on the masses of
black men puts skin color above justice and humanity.
These movements must be appraised as symptoms of
the profound frustration, despair, and impatience which
permeate all levels of Negro life in America and which
have come to the surface within recent years. They
cannot be dismissed as mere cults because the majority
of Negroes have so far not joined them. The psychological complexities from which these cults draw their
potential strength are shared by many Negroes on
various social and economic levels. A Negro manicurist
was quoted in a national magazine as saying: "You
know those Muslims are telling the truth about white
folks. I am not joining up, but I am not against them

either." Lorraine Hansberry, the well-known Negro playwright and one of the more militant younger intellectuals, wrote in a March 26 letter to the *New York Times:* " . . . I should not have hesitated to sit with, picket with, mourn with either Mustafa Bashire or Benjamin J. Davis or any other Negro who had the passion and understanding to be there [at the U.N. demonstration of Negro nationalist groups over Lumumba's death]. The continuation of intrigues against African and American Negro freedom demands high and steadfast unity among Negroes."

The resurgence of black nationalism among Negroes seems to be matched, if not counteracted, by an increasing critical evaluation of the basic structure, strength, and weaknesses of American society by a growing number of young Negro intellectuals. James Baldwin, novelist and essayist, is perhaps the outstanding example and the most eloquent of these younger Negro social critics. Baldwin says of the Black Muslims that they "do not expect anything at all from the white people of this country. They do not believe the American professions of democracy or equality have ever been remotely sincere. They insist on the total separation of the races." Baldwin states categorically that the fundamental appeal of the Black Muslims lies in the fact that they tell the *truth* about the plight of the Negro in America today. With bitter poignancy he states: "Usually, for example, those white people who are in favor of integration prove to be in favor of it later, in some other city, some other town, some other building, some other school. The rationalizations with which they attempt to disguise their panic cannot be respected.

"Northerners proffer their indignation about the South as a kind of badge, as proof of good intentions; they never suspect that they thus increase, in the heart of the Negro they address, a kind of helpless pain and rage — and pity."

In a bitter exclamation of futility and pessimism

Baldwin quotes a prominent Negro — "I am not at all
sure that I *want* to be integrated into a burning house."
He quotes another as saying "I might consider being
integrated into something else, an American society more
real and more honest — but *this?* No, thank you, man,
who *needs* it?"

That the pessimism stems from the general impatience
of the Negro and his awareness of and identification
with the swiftness of the changes taking place in Africa
is indicated by still another quote presented by Baldwin
— "At the rate things are going here, all of Africa will
be free before we can get a lousy cup of coffee."

A further indication of the present mood of the
younger Negro intellectual is the fact that he is directing his critical barbs not only at the inconsistencies and
injustices inherent in American racism but he is becoming increasingly critical — or more overt in his
criticisms — of traditional Negro leaders and Negro
organizations. While there have always been criticisms
of these individuals and organizations from the more
militant nationalistic groups of Negroes, it is significant
in appraising the present mood of the Negro, particularly in the North, to note the relatively new trend
wherein such criticisms, more reasoned and sober, are
now coming from a group of younger Negro intellectuals.

It is another index of the complexity of the present
level of strength and high morale of the Negro that
it is possible to view these criticisms as evidence that
the Negro in the North is now secure enough, on the
basis of his recent gains toward full and equal rights
as an American citizen, to assume the difficult role of
self-criticism and to demand that the Negro organizations become even more effective in obtaining complete
equality in the shortest possible time. The essence of
these criticisms is the heightened impatience of the
intellectual as his group nears the goal of full equality
and the insistence that the Negro organizations do not

compromise or settle for anything short of complete and immediate equality. His anxieties lest these organizations and leaders show signs of fatigue or politically expedient compromise place him at polar opposites to those whites who tend to see organizations like the NAACP as extremist groups. The impatient younger Negro is more likely to see these organizations as more moderate and conservative than is consistent with his own sense of urgency. An additional dimension of this paradox is found in the fact that, in spite of the sometimes hysterical criticisms of the NAACP by the more extremist nationalistic groups among Negroes, the more sober criticism from Negro intellectuals, and the strident, irrational criticisms and reprisals of white segregationists, the NAACP has increased its membership at an accelerated pace among Negroes in the North as well as in the South during the past decade.

Probably the most dramatic example of effective personal leadership among Negroes in recent years is the emergence of the Rev. Martin Luther King, Jr., as a symbol of the Negro's resistance to the stigma and humiliation of racial segregation. Rev. King's role in organizing, directing, and controlling the Montgomery bus boycott which culminated in a Supreme Court decision outlawing racial segregation in intrastate transportation catapulted him into national and international prominence. He captured the imagination of liberals and opponents of injustice throughout the world and justifiably won the loyalties and affection of American Negroes. The relationship between this type of leadership and the passive-resistance technique as used by Negro college students in the sit-ins and the freedom rides is clear in spite of the fact that King's role in the sit-ins and freedom rides was not one of direct leadership.

While Martin Luther King's initial impact among Negroes was indeed dramatic and national in scope, his type of personal leadership has been more effective in the South than in the North. The non-violent, passive-resistance, "love the oppressor" approach seems to have had some strategic effectiveness in the southern Negro's struggle against those specific and flagrant types of segregation and discrimination found in the South — on busses, in waiting rooms, and in other public accommodations. This philosophy and its related strategy and technique do not seem to be particularly appropriate in dealing with the more subtle forms of segregation and discrimination characteristic of northern communities. The selective buying campaign to expand employment opportunities among Negroes in Philadelphia seems to be the closest approach to the Martin Luther King technique found in effective use among northern Negroes. In general, however, patterns of discrimination in employment, political appointments, segregated housing, and de facto segregated schools do not seem to be easily dramatized by boycotts, sit-ins, or the strategic philosophy of "love of the oppressor." In fact, it is difficult in these cases to identify a specific oppressor even if one desired to "love" him into compliance with the laws of justice.

There are more subtle problems involved in attempting to appraise the over-all effect of Martin Luther King's philosophy in the long-range struggle of the Negro in America. On the obvious level, King's insistence that the Negro cannot afford to be corroded by hatred and must therefore discipline himself to love those who despise him is consistent with the Christian tradition and is the antithesis of the doctrine of hatred and racism preached by the black nationalists. On the surface, King's philosophy appears to reflect health and stability, while the black nationalists betray pathology and instability. A deeper analysis, however, might reveal that there is also an unrealistic, if not pathological, basis in King's doctrine. It is questionable whether the *masses* of an oppressed group can in fact "love" their oppressor. The natural reactions to injustice, oppression, and humiliation are bitterness and resentment. The form which such bitterness takes need not be overtly violent but the corrosion of the human spirit which is involved seems inevitable. It would seem, then, that any demand that the victims of oppression be required to love those who oppress them places an additional and probably intolerable psychological burden upon these victims.

It has been argued that the proper interpretation of King's philosophy of "love for the oppressor" must take into account its Christian philosophical and strategic significance. This argument may be perfectly correct for a small minority of educated and philosophically sophisticated individuals. But it is unlikely that it can be accepted with full understanding by the masses of Negroes. Their very attempt to cope with this type of philosophical abstraction in the face of the concrete injustices which dominate their daily lives could only lead to deep and disturbing inner conflicts and guilt. Finally, it is most disturbing to reflect on the possibility that this aspect of Martin Luther King's philosophy has received such widespread and uncritical acceptance among moderate and liberal whites because it is not inconsistent with the stereotype of the Negro as a meek, long-suffering creature who prays for deliverance but who rarely acts decisively against injustices.

There is no doubt that a new image of the Negro has emerged in the years following World War II. It might be desirable to restate for clarity the number of factors which have converged to make inevitable this demonstration of the Negro's impatient and ir- resistible demands for unqualified and immediate justice as a citizen in American democracy. Among these factors are the tremendous and rapid changes in our industrial and technological society, including miraculous new developments in transportation and communication; the massive migration of the Negro population from the southern to northern and western regions of the United States; the participation of Negroes in two major World Wars for democracy within this generation and their unwillingness to give their lives for democracy elsewhere while they are denied the benefits of democracy in their own land; the rise of communism as an aggressive ideological adversary of Western and American democratic ideology and the competitive struggle with this ideology for the loyalties of the people of the world; the rise of the independent states in Africa and Asia and the American Negro's identification with these people and his anxiety that with their increased status his own status as a rejected minority in his own land will become even more intolerable; the May 17, 1954, decision of the United States Supreme Court and its tremendous positive effect on the morale of the Negro; the dawdling, tortuously slow pace of desegregation in America and the equivocation and evasiveness of the legislative and executive branches of the federal government in dealing with problems of desegregation.

It is of psychological significance that the present impatience of the Negro and his unwillingness to accept any argument for the postponement of any of his rights as an American citizen reflect, among other things, the tremendous progress which has been made in race relations in America within the past twenty years. These real gains have whetted the Negro's appetite for the fruits of full equality as an American citizen without reservation, compromise, or postponement. The closer the Negro approaches these goals of full equality, the more impatient he becomes with existing forms of discrimination. The present posture of the American Negro may be most accurately characterized in terms of a rather stolid, persistent insistence upon his unqualified rights as an American citizen and a desire to assume the full responsibilities associated with such rights. He appears to be impatient with all equivocation, evasion, hypocrisy, and subterfuges which seek to postpone the fulfillment of these rights and responsibilities or to subordinate them to issues which are considered by others to be of greater importance. He sees problems of international relations, justice and democracy for others, the fight against communism, and problems of world peace as inextricably bound up with the problems of racial justice in America.

In fact the New Negro in the North as well as in the South has moved beyond the constricted level of mere racial protest and special pleading into the broader concern for strengthening the democratic foundations of America. He now recognizes beyond doubt that his destiny is one with the destiny of America and that he must contribute his thoughts and his strengths to increase the chances of America's survival and victory in its titanic struggle against a formidable adversary. To do so he must continue to demand that America demonstrate the validity and power and resilience of the democratic ideology by its ability to accept the Negro as a citizen without racial qualifications. The Negro cannot help America survive if America continues to exclude him from the necessary education, training, and dignity which are essential to human creativity.

It is the responsibility of the American Negro to free America from the shackles of racism and help his nation to reach that level of maturity and adaptability which is essential for its survival. The new image of the Negro and the responsibilities associated with this new image involve him in the role of social critic. In this role the American Negro demands that the fundamental moral values of democracy be established beyond the point of contamination. He cannot be content to demand integration and personal acceptance into a decaying moral structure. He cannot help his country gird itself for the arduous struggle before it by a willingness to share equally in a tottering structure of moral hypocrisy, social insensitivity, personal despair, and desperation. He must demand that the substance and strength inherent in the democratic process be fulfilled rather than cynically abused and disparaged.

The New Negro in the North has been forced by the

intricate complexities of world and national events to view himself and his struggles in the broader terms which go beyond regional boundaries or racial restrictions. His identification with the southern Negro is obvious, historic, and contemporaneous. His compassionate identification with the destiny of America is more recent but is a significant and imperative fact of our times. His identification with human beings throughout the world who are struggling to overthrow the yoke of past injustices and exploitations is increasingly clear. And his identification with all of mankind as it seeks solutions to the overriding problems of survival with justice and dignity is a significant fact of the present and one of the facts which determines the possibility of a future.

DIANE NASH

*was raised in Chicago
and went to the South for the
first time two years ago, when she enrolled in
Fisk University. Early in 1961 she became involved
in the Freedom Rides and interrupted her education to work
full-time for a year with the student sit-in and free-
dom-ride movement. At present she is
Coordinating Secretary for the
Nashville Non-Violent
Movement.*

INSIDE THE SIT-INS AND

FREEDOM RIDES: TESTIMONY

OF A SOUTHERN STUDENT

I see no alternative but that this text must be a personal interpretation of my own experience within the region known as "Dixie."

My participation in the movement began in February, 1960, with the lunch counter "sit-ins." I was then a student at Fisk University, but several months ago I interrupted my schoolwork for a year in order to work full time with the movement. My occupation at present is coordinating secretary for the Nashville Nonviolent Movement.

I should not wish to infer that I speak for the southern movement, for I think that there is no single person who can do that. Although many of the following statements can be generalized for the entire movement in the South, I shall refer largely to Nashville, Tennessee, for that is where I have worked.

I submit, then, that the nonviolent movement in that city:

1. is based upon and motivated by love;
2. attempts to serve God and mankind;
3. strives toward what we call the beloved community.

This is religion. This is applied religion. I think it has worked for me and I think it has worked for you and I think it is the work of our Church.

One fact occurs to me. This is that the problems of the world lie within men and women; yes, within you, me, and the people with whom we come in contact daily. Further, the problems lie not so much in our action as in our inaction. We have upon ourselves as individuals in a democracy the political, economic, sociological, and spiritual responsibilities of our country. I'm wondering now if we in the United States are really remembering that this must be a government "of the people" and "by the people" as well as "for the people." Are we really appreciating the fact that if you and I do not meet these responsibilities then our government *cannot* survive as a democracy?

The problems in Berlin, Cuba, or South Africa are, I think, identical with the problem in Jackson, Mississippi, or Nashville, Tennessee. I believe that when men come to believe in their own dignity and in the worth of their own freedom, and when they can acknowledge the God and the dignity that is within every man, then Berlin and Jackson will not be problems. After I had been arrested from a picket line about three weeks ago, I jotted down the following note, with this meeting in mind:

> If the policeman had acknowledged the God within each of the students with whom I was arrested last night, would he have put us in jail? Or would he have gone into the store we were picketing and tried to persuade the manager to hire Negroes and to treat all people fairly? If one acknowledges the God within men, would anyone ask for a "cooling off period," or plead for gradualism, or would they realize that white and Negro Americans are committing sin every day that they hate each other and every day that they allow an evil system to exist without doing all they can to rectify it as soon as they can?

Segregation reaches into every aspect of life to oppress the Negro and to rob him of his dignity in the South. The very fact that he is forced to be separated obviously implies his inferiority. Therefore the phrase "separate but equal" denies itself. The things non-black

Americans take for granted, such as a movie and dinner date for college students, or a coffee-break downtown, are usually denied the black American in the South. Sometimes he may obtain these services if he wishes to compromise his dignity. He might, for example, attend a downtown movie if he would enter through the alley entrance and climb to the balcony to be seated.

But these are not the most important things. The purpose of the movement and of the sit-ins and the Freedom Rides and any other such actions, as I see it, is to bring about a climate in which all men are respected as men, in which there is appreciation of the dignity of man and in which each individual is free to grow and produce to his fullest capacity. We of the movement often refer to this goal as the concept of the redeemed or the "beloved" community.

In September, 1959, I came to Nashville as a student at Fisk University. This was the first time that I had been as far south as Tennessee; therefore, it was the first time that I had encountered the blatant segregation that exists in the South. I came then to see the community in sin. Seeing signs designating "white" or "colored," being told, "We don't serve niggers in here," and, as happened in one restaurant, being looked in the eye and told, "Go around to the back door where you belong," had a tremendous psychological impact on me. To begin with, I didn't agree with the premise that I was inferior, and I had a difficult time complying with it. Also, I felt stifled and boxed in since so many areas of living were restricted. The Negro in the South is told constantly, "You can't sit here." "You can't work there." "You can't live here, or send your children to school there." "You can't use this park, or that swimming pool," and on and on and on. Restrictions extend into housing, schools, jobs (Negroes, who provide a built-in lower economic class, are employed in the most menial capacities and are paid the lowest wages). Segregation encompasses city parks, swimming pools and recreational facilities, lunch counters, restaurants, movies, drive-in movies, drive-in restaurants, restrooms, water fountains, bus terminals, train stations, hotels, motels, auditoriums (Negro college students usually attend the most important formal dances of the year in the school gymnasium), amusement parks, legitimate theatres, bowling alleys, skating rinks — all of these areas are segregated. Oppression extends to every area of life.

In the deeper South, Negroes are denied use of public libraries, they are denied entrance even to certain department stores, are discriminated against on city buses, in taxicabs, and in voting. Failure to comply with these oppressions results in beatings, in house-burnings and bombings, and economic reprisals, as we saw in Fayette County, Tennessee, and in Montgomery in the case of the Freedom Riders. Significant, however, are the many countless incidents that the public never even hears about.

As can easily be imagined, all this has a real effect upon the Negro. I won't attempt to analyze here the effect of the system upon the Negro, but I should like to make a few observations. An organism must make some type of adjustment to its environment. The Negro, however, continues to deny consciously to himself, and to his children, that he is inferior. Yet each time he uses a "colored" facility, he testifies to his own inferiority. Many of the values that result from this dual self-concept are amazing to note. Let me relate to you one very interesting incident.

I spent thirty days in the jail in Rock Hill, South Carolina. For the first few days the heat was intense in the cell. Breathing was difficult. Everyone was perspiring profusely. We couldn't understand why the women in the cell hesitated to ask that a window be opened or the heat be turned down. It turned out that it was because they were so often cold in their homes, and had come to value heat so highly, that they were willing to suffer from it if they could just have it.

A further example of these curious values is given
by the Negro who has received several college degrees
or who has a profession and who can consider himself
a successful and important man, but who, at the same
time, will still attest to his own inferiority by cooperating
with segregation. What value, or lack of it, accounts for
the fact that so many faculty members at Negro colleges
have not disassociated themselves from universities
which have expelled student demonstrators? Why are
the faculty members and administrators of southern
Negro colleges not on the picket lines and sitting at the
lunch counters? I think the answer lies within the answer
of what Jim Crow does to the Negro. For one thing, it
stymies his ability to be free by placing emphasis on
the less important things, but on things, nevertheless,
which Negroes have been denied.

Segregation has its destructive effect upon the segregator also. The most outstanding of these effects perhaps
is fear. I can't forget how openly this fear was displayed
in Nashville on the very first day that students there
sat-in. Here were Negro students, quiet, in good discipline, who were consciously attempting to show no ill
will, even to the point of making sure that they had
pleasant and calm facial expressions. The demonstrators
did nothing more than sit on the stools at the lunch
counter. Yet, from the reaction of the white employees
of the variety stores and from the onlookers, some dread-
ful monster might just as well have been about to devour
them all. Waitresses dropped things. Store managers and
personnel perspired. Several cashiers were led off in
tears. One of the best remembered incidents of that day
took place in a ladies restroom of a department store.
Two Negro students, who had sat-in at the lunch counter,
went into the ladies restroom which was marked "white"
and were there as a heavy-set, older white lady, who
might have been seeking refuge from the scene taking
place at the lunch counter, entered. Upon opening the
door and finding the two Negro girls inside, the woman

threw up her hands and, nearly in tears, exclaimed, "Oh! Nigras everywhere!"

So segregation engenders fear in the segregator, especially needless fear of what will happen if integration comes; in short, fear of the unknown. Then Jim Crow fosters ignorance. The white person is denied the educational opportunities of exchange with people of a race other than his own. Bias makes for the hatred which we've all seen stamped upon the faces of whites in newspaper pictures of the mob. The white hoodlum element is often provoked and egged on by the management or by onlookers; this is a type of degradation into which the segregator unfortunately slips.

Police departments can also sink to a sorry state. Bias lets the police turn their heads and not see the attacks made against demonstrators. In Nashville, police permissiveness has served to make the hoodlum element more and more bold, with incidents of real seriousness resulting, even a real tragedy, as was the case in the bombing of a Negro attorney's home last year during the sit-ins.

An unhappy result of segregation is that communications between the races become so limited as to be virtually nonexistent. The "good race relations" to which segregators in the South often refer, is nothing more than a complete breakdown in communication so that one race is not aware of any of the other race's objections or of interracial problems. This has been clearly exemplified in cities where race relations have been called "good" and where the masses of Negroes have rallied behind students in boycotts of downtown areas that have been, reportedly, up to 98 per cent effective among the Negro population.

By not allowing all its citizens to produce and contribute to the limit of their capacities, the entire city, or region, or country, will suffer, as can be seen in the South's slow progress in industrial, political, and other areas today and in the weakening of American influence abroad as a result of race hatred.

Segregation, moreover, fosters dishonesty between the races. It makes people lie to each other. It allows white merchants to accept the customers' money, but to give them unequal service, as at the Greyhound and Trailway Bus Lines, where all customers pay the same fares but some are not free to use all the facilities in the terminals and at restaurants where rest stops are made. Fares are equal, but service is not. The system forces the Negro maid to tell her employer that everything is all right and that she's satisfied, but when she is among her friends she talks about the injustice of the system.

Worst of all, however, is the stagnancy of thought and character — of both whites and Negroes — which is the result of the rationalization that is necessary in order that the oppressed and oppressor may live with a system of slavery and human abasement.

I can remember Nashville in this stage of sin when I first came there in September, 1959, a few months before the sit-in movement was to begin. As a new student at Fisk University that September, I was completely unaware that over the next few months I would really experience segregation; that I would see raw hatred; that I would see my friends beaten; that I would be a convict several times and, as is the case at the moment, that there would be a warrant out for my arrest in Jackson, Mississippi. Expecting my life to pursue a rather quiet course, I was also unaware that I would begin to feel part of a group of people suddenly proud to be called "black." To be called "Negro" had once been thought of as derogatory and had been softened by polite company to "colored person." At one time, to have been called "nigger" was a gross insult and hurt keenly. Within the movement, however, we came to a realization of our own worth. We began to see our role and our responsibility to our country and to our fellow men, so

that to be called "nigger" on the picket line, or anywhere, was now an unimportant thing that no longer
produced in us that flinch. As to the typical white southerner who compromises with "nigra" we only secretly
wish for a moment when we could gracefully help him
with his phonetics, explaining that it's "knee — grow."

The revolution in the Negro student's concept of the
name of his own race is really important only as it is
indicative of change in the Negro's concept of himself
and of his race.

Through the unity and purposefulness of the experience of the Nashville Negro, there was born a new awareness of himself as an individual.

There was also born, on the part of whites, a new
understanding and awareness of the Negro as a person
to be considered and respected.

I think an outstanding example of this latter change
was revealed by the negotiations which took place between Negro students and leaders and the white merchants who were the managers of downtown lunch
counters. It became apparent to me during the negotiations that the white southerner was not in the habit
of taking the Negro seriously. During the initial stages,
the attitude of the merchants was one of sort of patting
us on the head and saying, "Yes, we've listened to your
story and maybe segregation is bad, but you can't have
integration now, because it'll ruin our business." And
they closed the matter there. However, after the sit-ins
continued and after the moral weight of the community
was felt, through our 98 per cent effective boycott; after
a number of talks in which the merchants got to know
us as people and saw our problem (and we saw theirs),
there was indeed a beautiful type of awareness born, to
the extent that one of the merchants, who incidentally
was a white southerner, made what I think was a real
concession: "Well, it was simply that we didn't see they
were right and we were wrong."

I think we can also see this awareness of Negro and

white for each other as individuals, in the attitudes of the crowds who watched the demonstrations. In the beginning, as I mentioned, there was mostly fear. However, after the violence was allowed to go on and after the police protection broke down and officers insisted on looking the other way while people were beaten, not infrequently there was a white person in the crowd who would see someone about to tear up one of the picket signs or about to hit someone, and would go up and stop this person and say, "No, no! You can't do that." And often they would get into a discussion which sometimes looked constructive. I hope it was.

There also has been a real change in the temper of the crowd, a change from fear to, I think, just curiosity and watching because something is going on. There is not the hatred and the serious fear and emotional tension that there once was. In Nashville, since the integration of the lunch counters and dining rooms and department stores, we've been fortunate enough to have movies also integrated. As I mentioned earlier, in the downtown area Negroes could not attend movies unless they entered through an alley entrance and sat in the balcony. However, after several weeks of standing-in, they are now allowed to use the theatres' facilities on a fully integrated basis.

Swimming pools in Nashville have been closed this summer under very strange circumstances. It seems that on one particular day a group of Negroes attempted to integrate the city's swimming pools, which incidentally, of course, are tax-supported. On the next day, the park commissioners closed all the swimming pools in the city, for financial reasons. Now it seems that the mayor did not know anything about the park commission being in serious financial difficulty, nor did any of the other city officials, and strangely enough the park commissioners could not be reached for comment. But I'm afraid our swimming pools are closed for financial reasons.

The H. G. Hill food stores are currently being picketed. This is our local project for the moment. This company hires Negroes only for warehouse work and as truck drivers and, of course, pays them below union standards. Many stores are in completely Negro neighborhoods and even in these stores we cannot have Negro cashiers or personnel.

I am eager to talk with you about the Freedom Rides because I think that they denote a new and important level of effort. And I feel that more such projects will be necessary for the ultimate success of the southern movement, especially in states of the deep South, such as Alabama and Mississippi. As you know, the idea of a Freedom Ride was conceived and the project was begun by the Congress of Racial Equality. The first trip originated in Washington, D. C., in May of this year (1961). From Washington, the group traveled through most of the southern states and was repeatedly beaten and jailed as the bus made its way across Dixie. As you remember, at Anniston and Birmingham, Alabama, the bus met with mob violence; the CORE members were beaten and the bus was burned. Most of the riders were hospitalized for a short time. Mr. James Peck, who was one of the whites along with the group, had fifty stitches taken in his head as a result of the repeated beatings that he had to take. Attempting to get a bus to their destination, which was Montgomery, the riders were told that no driver would take them further. In a state of exhaustion then, after traveling hundreds of miles under tremendous tension, repeated jailings and beatings, they took a plane to New Orleans, which was the last stop of the planned itinerary.

In Nashville, the students had been closely following the Freedom Bus as it moved from town to town, for the people on the bus somehow were ourselves. Their dream of freedom in travel was our dream also. Their aspirations were our own aspirations. There is a tremendous bond between people who really stand up or ride for what they feel is just and right. You see, the

CORE members were riding and being beaten for our freedom, too. Therefore, it was quite simple. Mob violence must not stop men's striving toward right. Freedom Rides and other such actions must not be stopped until our nation is really free.

In Nashville then, we were faced with a grave situation. We called a meeting of the students and adults within the movement. Talking by phone with persons who had been at the scene of the tragedies in Birmingham and Anniston, we were told, "Don't come. It's a bloodbath. Be assured, someone will be killed if you do come." Upon hearing this, the Nashville group set about preparing themselves for the fact that someone of them would be killed when they took the trip.

You see, these people faced the probability of their own deaths before they ever left Nashville. Several made out wills. A few more gave me sealed letters to be mailed if they were killed. Some told me frankly that they were afraid, but they knew that this was something that they must do because freedom was worth it. I, incidentally, feel very blessed and very grateful for knowing such people and for being able to call most of them my friends.

The purpose of any nonviolent demonstration is to focus the attention of people on how evil segregation really is and then to change their hearts. Some people have been confused about the objectives of the Freedom Rides, and I've heard it said that "the point has been made," so there is no use in going on. The objective of the Freedom Ride from Birmingham was not just to point out that people cannot ride freely but to make it possible for all persons to ride and use terminal facilities without being discriminated against. Until that objective has been attained there *is* reason for going on.

So the drama continued. The bus left Nashville about 6:00 A.M. en route to Birmingham, Alabama. My own role was to stay at the telephone, to keep contact with Birmingham, to hear from the riders as often as they could call, to make arrangements ahead in Montgomery, to keep the Justice Department advised — in short, to co-ordinate.

The students were held on the bus for some time when they reached Birmingham, and subsequently were taken into "protective custody." The next morning at 4:25, I received a call from them. They said that they'd been driven by the police to the Alabama-Tennessee border and had been put out of the car there on the highway and told to cross the border. At the moment they were on the open highway and felt unsafe. They did not know where shelter was, but would call again as soon as possible. They had been fasting since they had been in jail the day before.

We immediately sent an automobile to get them, and the next time we heard from them, they advised us that they were returning to Birmingham and were determined to board a bus for Montgomery. The police chief wasn't going to get off that easily.

The next night was an all-night vigil for them at the bus station. They were told, again, that no driver would drive the bus. Finally, next morning they were able to get a driver and the bus moved on to Montgomery, Alabama. We all read about that morning, I think, in Montgomery, Alabama. I wish I could have shared with you the moments in our office when that violence was taking place. It seemed that when the bus arrived and the mob attacked the students, they were immediately dispersed. People put a few of them in their cars and took them home. Within a very short time the group was scattered throughout the city.

We listed all the names of the persons who had left Nashville and began trying to account for them. We would ask the students as they called in, "When did you last see ....?" The reports we got that morning were: John Lewis was bleeding profusely from the head; another student seemed unconscious; Jim Swirg had been cornered by about sixteen or seventeen men and was being beaten. They had lead pipes, knives, and guns. In a relatively short time, however, we were able to account for all of the students. Miraculously, no one was dead.

Shortly afterwards, in the job of coordinator, I went down to Montgomery to help with the work there. I think you probably read about the meeting which took place in the church in Montgomery that night, at which Martin Luther King, the Freedom Riders, and a number of other people were present. When the police would not afford the church protection, a car was burned. There were incidents of violence and a mob of thousands, I understand, gathered outside. People in the church that night didn't know how close they were to real tragedy. This was the night martial law was declared in Montgomery. That night everyone remained in the church throughout the night.

Now something very interesting took place in the church that night. I think it can almost be a generalization that the Negroes in Alabama and Mississippi and elsewhere in the deep South are terribly afraid until they get into the movement. In the dire danger in which we were that night, no one expressed anything except concern for freedom and the thought that someday we'll be free. We stayed there until dawn and everyone was naturally tired, but no one said so. There were about three thousand people there that night, representing all walks of life, from young children to the elder people in the community. I don't think I've ever seen a group of people band together as the crowd in the church did that night.

Finally at dawn, we were escorted home by the troops. The students boarded the bus for Jackson, along with a second bus that had come from Nashville carrying five ministers. The buses left for Jackson, Mississippi, and I think we pretty well know the story from there on. Immediately upon arrival, the people were jailed. Since

then there have been roughly three hundred people jailed
for doing nothing more than riding a bus.

It interests me that the Freedom Riders have been
called "trouble makers," "seekers of violence," and "seekers of publicity." Few people have seen the point: here
are people acting within their constitutional and moral
rights; they have done nothing more than ride a bus or
use a facility that anyone else would normally expect to
use any day of the year, but they have been confined
and imprisoned for it. And somehow the Attorney General and the President of the United States and the Justice Department of the United States can do nothing
about such a gross injustice. As far as being seekers of
violence and publicity, the students have, at all times,
remained non-violent. Are not the committers of violence responsible for their own actions? To date, as I've
said, there have been approximately three hundred people jailed as Freedom Riders. All were returned within
the last two weeks for arraignment. There stood to be
lost five hundred dollars for each person who did not
return to Jackson. And out of 189 who were on bond,
all except nine were returned. The riders had been convicted in the city court and are currently appealing on
the county court level. Their appeal trials have been
set at the rate of two per day between now and January.
The first trial took place yesterday. The result of that
trial is that Mr. Henry Thomas was convicted of breach
of peace, sentenced to four months imprisonment, and
his bond was set at two thousand dollars.

Now I think that this is a serious question for the
American public to consider. Is this really the country
in which we live? This is a serious moment, I think, for
those who take democracy and freedom seriously. Remember now that these Freedom Riders are citizens of
the United States who can be called on to go to war and
who are receiving treatment of this type.

If so harsh a treatment is involved for an action as
right as riding a bus, perhaps one as unimportant as

riding a bus, can we not draw from that an inference of what life in the South for the Negro must really be like?

I think that it is most essential that the government move at a rate of progress adequate to meet the needs of the governed. Not being able to do so has resulted in the tragedies of Little Rock, New Orleans, and Montgomery. It might be interesting to note that we have not had incidents such as New Orleans and Montgomery where there has been adequate government. There always needs to be a Faubus or a Patterson.

The Negro must be represented by those who govern. Without this representation, there is moral slavery, if not physical. No person or country can have a clear conscience and a noble mien with such a sin on its conscience. I'm interested now in the people who call for gradualism. The answer, it seems to me, is to stop sinning and stop now! How long must we wait? It's been a century. How gradual can you get? Montgomery has shown how far it has advanced on its own; we've seen this from the mob to the governor. As for the legal position about the right to serve whom one pleases, I would say that this position does not alter the fact that segregation is wrong. Segregation on the bus lines, trains, and planes is wrong *intra*state as well as *inter*state. The press has made much of the interstate passage. However, the Freedom Riders are just as concerned with intrastate travel, because we're concerned with the injustice of segregation.

The Negro is seeking to take advantage of the opportunities that society offers; the same opportunities that others take for granted, such as a cup of coffee at Woolworth's, a good job, an evening at the movies, and dignity. Persons favoring segregation often refer to the rights of man, but they never mention the rights of Negro men.

I would like to say also that the students and the adults who have taken part in this movement and who are doing so now are dead serious. We're ready to give our lives. It is a slight miracle, I think, that in the almost two years since February of 1960 there has not been a fatality. But we have come amazingly close to it several times. Let me mention the case of William Barbee who was on the Freedom Ride when it arrived at Montgomery and met with mob violence. Barbee had gone on a few hours ahead to arrange for cars and other necessities before the riders arrived. When they did get there and were attacked, he was busy trying to get them into taxi cabs or ambulances and take them where they could receive medical attention. Just as about all of them had gotten into cabs, the mob attacked him.

At that moment a Negro man was passing by. He was on his way to pay a bill. It was just a regular day in his life until he saw one of the mobsters with his foot upon William Barbee's neck. Mr. Nichols, who had lived in the South all his life, said that he started to go ahead about his business. But, he said, he knew that he would never be able to live with his conscience again if that man killed Barbee. So he turned around and pulled the man off. Well, Mr. Nichols landed in the hospital next to Barbee. But even after he had pulled the man off, the crowd went back to William Barbee, and he was again in danger of death when the head of the highway patrol came along and was able to get the mob off with a gun. This student, William Barbee, is back in the movement, has been beaten up on a picket line and jailed again. I think that this is indicative of some of the determination and the seriousness with which we take the cause.

I think that quite often today you can hear the strains of a very old spiritual that's sung quite seriously. Some of the words are: "Before I be a slave I would be buried in my grave and go home to My Lord and be free."

From those who say they approve the ends, not the means, I would be interested in suggestions for a means which would yield freedom without delay. Let us look at the means. The students have chosen non-violence as a technique; there is no reason why they couldn't have taken up guns. It was a responsible choice, I think. We have decided that if there is to be suffering in this revolution (which is really what the movement is — a revolution), we will take the suffering upon ourselves and never inflict it upon our fellow man, because we respect him and recognize the God within him.

Let us see now what the movement needs. The movement is very much in need of a major federal decision that will result in enforcement of the Constitution and federal law. (You might be interested to know that during the Freedom Rides Governor Ross Barnett of Mississippi informed me of two very interesting things by telephone: He said (1) that he did not feel that Supreme Court decisions applied to his state, and (2) that he intended to enforce Mississippi law over and above any federal law that conflicted with it.) Along with a major federal decision to follow through on civil rights, there is needed a major decision on the part of the people. There is needed a realization that the problem lies as much in Jackson or Nashville as it does in Berlin or anywhere in the world. The problem, I think, centers around the questions of truth, honesty, justice, and democracy. What is needed is concern for human rights — not just white human rights. Until such time as this realization comes, Freedom Rides and similar such south-wide projects are necessary. Count on more of them.

As far as the Catholic student and the Catholic Church are concerned, from our pulpits we need directness and we need emphasis. If this is not an area in which the Church must work, what is? It seems that our role must necessarily be leadership. And anything but outspoken and direct leadership in this movement is immoral. Newman Clubs and campus organizations in the South can certainly revitalize themselves by contacting local movements or starting one, pledging their support and participation. And the same is true for the problems which exist in the North.

There are roles for all of us to play. First, of course, is the role of the participant, who really pickets or sits in. Then there is the role of the observer. I don't know if you have heard, but a number of whites are being utilized effectively as observers. In the integration of lunch counters and movie theaters, many of the older church women who have been sympathetic with the cause for a long time, but who haven't had an opportunity to speak out, have helped by doing such things as sitting next to Negroes at the lunch counters or at movies and thus creating an appearance of normalcy. These people have become quite enthusiastic about their new role. There have been several cases of — well, real "bigness." One lady is known to have drunk countless cups of coffee and gained ten pounds in sitting at lunch counters all day for several days in a row and looking normal. Several have been known to see the same picture over and over again. Also looking normal. For those in the North, as I mentioned, there are local problems, and we also need groups that we can call upon to support the southern movement.

Finally, this movement has been called one of passive resistance. But it is not that at all. Rather it might be called one of active insistence. In regard to our own roles and the role of our Church, I think we need to understand that this is a question of *real* love of man and love of God. Is there such a thing as moderate love of God or moderate disdain for sin? I think we need radical good to combat radical evil. Consider the South. It can be the answer for the free world; it can be the pivot. The problem there is a vital challenge for truth; for respect for man. In a word, it is a question of dignity.

WILLIAM J. KENEALY, S.J.
*is Visiting Professor
of Law at the Loyola University
in Chicago. A member of the American Bar Association and the American Judicature
Society, he has contributed to various legal periodicals on
the subjects of legal philosophy, constitutional law, and civil
liberties. Father Kenealy has been Chairman of the
National Conference of Jesuit Law Schools and is
presently Chaplain for the North Suburban Chapter of the Catholic
Interracial Council of
Chicago.*

THE LEGALITY
OF THE SIT-INS

These familiar words of the Declaration of Independence, written in 1776, are not part of the organic law of the land:

> We hold these truths to be self-evident: that all men are created equal; that they are endowed by their Creator with certain inalienable rights; that among these are life, liberty, and the pursuit of happiness; that to secure these rights, governments are instituted among men, deriving their just powers from the consent of the governed.

They express, however, the vitalizing spirit which generated the body of our Federal Constitution of 1789 and our Bill of Rights of 1791. They epitomize the living philosophy of our law and of our democratic government. They illuminate the meaning, as indeed they inspired the text, of the preamble to our Federal Constitution:

> We, the people of the United States, in order to form a more perfect union, establish justice, insure domestic tranquillity, provide for the common defense, promote the general welfare, and secure the blessings of liberty to ourselves and our posterity, do ordain and establish this Constitution for the United States of America.

This is the public philosophy upon which this nation was founded and to which this nation by its most solemn covenants is dedicated. I will not elaborate the fact that this public philosophy is based squarely upon the *philosophia perennis* of the natural law.[1] I will not develop the fact that this public philosophy is completely consonant with Catholic theology which embraces the natural law.[2] Suffice it to say that, despite the cynics in some academic halls and the secularists on some public platforms, the glory of the American Constitution is that, for the first time in history, a great and powerful people, in a solemn profession of *politico-religious* faith, made human dignity, human freedom, and human equality under God, the cornerstones of its political and constitutional structure.

But ideals are not enough. They must be put to work. General principles alone do not solve particular problems. Neither a philosophy nor a constitution is self-executing. A constitution demands legislative implementation, judicial interpretation, and executive enforcement. Moreover, it may need amendment from time to time, as the conditions and circumstances of social life change, and as experience and maturity discover truth and disclose error.

In most respects, the Constitution of 1789 was a magnificent and dynamic document. But it was not written in heaven. It was by no means perfect. Since it was amended by the Bill of Rights in 1791, thirteen other amendments have been added from 1798 to 1961. It will undoubtedly be amended in the future. And if the ideals of human dignity, human freedom, and human equality under God cannot be realized practically under the Constitution as presently amended, then it must be amended in the future. The history of constitutional development is enlightening.

---

1. Kenealy, "Racism, Law and Politics," delivered before the National Catholic Conference for Interracial Justice, August 25, 1960; reprinted in *Interracial Review*, November, 1960, p. 256.

2. *Ibid.*, p. 278.

Despite the solemn profession of the equality of man under God, enunciated in the Declaration of Independence, some of the Founding Fathers were slave-owners. Despite the solemn purpose to secure the blessings of liberty, set out in its preamble, the original Constitution of 1789 provided for human slavery without limitation of time, protected the slave trade until 1808, and required the return of fugitive slaves to their owners:

> *Art. I, Sec. 2, §3:* Representatives and direct Taxes shall be apportioned among the several States which may be included within this Union, according to their respective Numbers, which shall be determined by adding to the whole Number of free Persons, including those bound to Service for a Term of Years, and excluding Indians not taxed, three fifths of all other Persons [i.e., slaves].

> *Art. I, Sec. 9, §1:* The Migration or Importation of Such Persons [slaves] as any of the States now existing shall think proper to admit, shall not be prohibited by the Congress prior to the Year one thousand eight hundred and eight....

> *Art. IV, Sec. 2, §3:* No Person held to Service or Labour in one State, under the Laws thereof [slaves], escaping into another, shall, in Consequence of any Law or Regulation therein, be discharged from such Service or Labour, but shall be delivered up on Claim of the Party to whom such Service or Labour may be due.

The deficiencies of the original Constitution of 1789, and a widespread fear of the possible abuse of the "necessary and proper" clause of Article I, Section 8, created an immediate popular demand for a federal Bill of Rights. Although many, including James Madison, argued that a specific Bill of Rights was unnecessary, since the new federal government was one of limited and delegated powers, nevertheless the popular insistence led to the drafting and the ratification of the first ten amendments in 1791. The first eight are known as the Bill of Rights.

The Bill of Rights of 1791 was a limitation of the powers of the new federal government only, and not of the powers of the sovereign states. The personal rights enumerated were protected against federal action only, and not against state action. This common understanding was confirmed by the Supreme Court in 1833 in *Barron v. Baltimore*,[3] a case involving an alleged taking, by Maryland, of private property without just compensation. It was again confirmed by the Court in 1845 in *Permoli v. New Orleans*,[4] a case involving an alleged denial, by Louisiana, of the free exercise of religion. In the latter case, a unanimous Court declared:

> The Constitution makes no provision for protecting the citizens of the respective States in their religious liberties; this is left to the state constitutions and laws; nor is there any inhibition imposed by the Constitution of the United States in this respect on the States.

As the Bill of Rights did not protect the fundamental personal rights of citizens against state action, a fortiori it did not protect non-citizens against the savage abomination of human slavery sanctioned by state laws. The Bill of Rights did not, and was not intended to, amend the provisions of the original Constitution concerning slavery, the slave trade, or the return of fugitive slaves. Moreover, there was no significant popular demand, at that time, to do anything about slavery.

How could that be? The Founding Fathers were not gross hypocrites. The people of the time were not moral monsters. Profoundly influenced by the customs and traditions of their time (as, indeed, all of us are), partially blinded by the persuasiveness of property (a trait not uncommon today), considerably compromised by the bitter practicalities of sectional politics (a perennial problem), they simply failed to appreciate to the full, and to execute in practice, the majestic philosophy enunciated in the Declaration of Independence and in the preamble

3. 7 Pet. 243 (1833).
4. 3 How. 589 (1845).

to the Constitution. As Chief Justice Taney said, in the tragic case of *Dred Scott v. Sanford*:[5]

> It is difficult at this day [1857] to realize the state of public opinion in relation to that unfortunate [Negro] race, which prevailed in the civilized and enlightened portions of the world at the time of the Declaration of Independence, and when the Constitution of the United States was adopted. . . . They [the Negroes] had for more than a century been regarded as beings of an inferior order; and altogether unfit to associate with the white race, either in social or political relations; and so far inferior, that they had no rights which the white man was bound to respect; and that the negro might justly and lawfully be reduced to slavery for his benefit.

A year after the Dred Scott decision, on December 18, 1858, Abraham Lincoln is reported to have opened his fourth debate with Stephen A. Douglas with remarks which have been widely quoted by modern segregationists:

> I will say then that I am not, nor ever have been, in favor of bringing about in any way the social and political equality of the white and black races . . . there is a physical difference between the races which will forever forbid the two races living together on terms of social and political equality.

Four years after this political debate, on August 14, 1862, President Lincoln is reported to have addressed the first group of free Negroes ever to visit the White House in response to a presidential invitation, with expressions which have also been frequently quoted by twentieth century racists:

> Whether it is right or wrong I need not discuss; but this physical difference [between the races] is a great disadvantage to us both. . . . But for your race among us there could not be a war, although many men en-

---

5. 19 How. 393, 15 L. Ed. 691 (1857).

gaged on either side do not care for you one way or
the other. Nevertheless, I repeat, without the institution
of slavery, and the colored race as a basis, the war
could not have an existence. It is better for us both,
therefore, to be separated.

I have a profound reverence for Washington, Jeffer-
son, Hamilton, and Lincoln. I am sincerely inspired by
the tremendous positive achievements of the Founding
Fathers and of the Great Emancipator. But I do not
deify them. They were great men, but not divine. They
were wise men, but not infallible. And I confess to an
intellectual impatience with patriotic and political
speeches, in or out of partisan conventions, fervently
and uncritically urging me to *return* to the Founding
Fathers or to the Great Emancipator. It is given to
nations as well as men to grow, and not merely in age
and size, but in wisdom and grace as well. Wherefore,
in the growth and perfection of American democracy
and the realization of American ideals, I think it is imperative that we proceed, not *back* to the Founding
Fathers or the Great Emancipator, but *forward* from
their mighty achievements. Thank God, we have done
so to a considerable extent. We have not been entirely
shackled by a blind and unreasoning adherence to all
the injustices of the past. The principles of the Declaration of Independence, the philosophy of the natural
law, and the teachings of Christ are clearer now in the
national conscience. We have caught a glimpse, at least,
of a better future.

After the tragic Dred Scott decision in 1857, which
helped to plunge a bitterly divided nation into a fratri-
cidal civil war, President Lincoln's Emancipation Proclamation in 1863, the Thirteenth Amendment in 1865, the
Fourteenth in 1868, and the Fifteenth in 1870, destroyed
forever the barbarism of human slavery in the United
States, and swept the nation *forward* in giant strides
from the status quo of the Founding Fathers in the direction of human dignity, practical liberty, and genuine

equality for all men under God. We did advance in wisdom. We did grow in grace. The constitutional evidence is worth reviewing:

> *Amendment XIII, Sec. 1:* Neither slavery nor involuntary servitude, except as a punishment for crime whereof the party shall have been duly convicted, shall exist within the United States, or any place subject to their jurisdiction.

> *Amendment XIV, Sec. 1:* All persons born or naturalized in the United States, and subject to the jurisdiction thereof, are citizens of the United States and of the State wherein they reside. No State shall make or enforce any law which shall abridge the privileges or immunities of citizens of the United States; nor shall any State deprive any person of life, liberty, or property, without due process of law; nor deny to any person within its jurisdiction the equal protection of the laws.

> *Amendment XV, Sec. 1:* The right of citizens of the United States to vote shall not be denied or abridged by the United States or by any State on account of race, color, or previous condition of servitude.

These three Civil War amendments nullified the Supreme Court decisions in *Barron v. Baltimore, Permoli v. New Orleans,* and *Dred Scott v. Sanford.* Not because they changed the Bill of Rights. They did not. The Bill of Rights remains as a limitation on federal power. But because they set up some new limitations on both federal and state power. As against both federal and state power, they outlawed human slavery, granted citizenship to Negroes, and guaranteed the citizens' right to vote. As against state power, they protected the privileges and immunities of United States citizens, due process of law, and the equal protection of the laws. They empowered the federal courts, for the first time, to protect all fundamental personal rights *against state action.* This was tremendous progress. Many of the framers and ratifiers of these amendments believed and hoped that they had finally abolished, not merely the substance and accidents of Negro slavery, but all forms of racial discrimination and degradation. But their hopes were doomed to frustration.

Two critical decisions of the Supreme Court blocked the full realization of Negro freedom and equality: the *Civil Rights Cases* of 1883[6] and *Plessy v. Ferguson* in 1896.[7] The first of these decisions is still the law of the land, the latter has been overruled by the *School Segregation Cases* of 1954[8] and subsequent supporting cases. For convenience sake I shall speak of *Plessy v. Ferguson* first.

In 1896 the Supreme Court in *Plessy v. Ferguson* decided that the "equal protection of the laws" clause of the Fourteenth Amendment was satisfied by a Louisiana statute which required railroads in that state to provide "equal but separate" facilities for the white and colored races; and, consequently, that compulsory racial segregation was constitutional. The decision was not unanimous. Justice John Marshall Harlan, the grandfather of the present Justice Harlan, wrote a powerful and prophetic dissent. Arguing that "there is no caste here . . . our Constitution is color-blind and neither knows nor tolerates classes among citizens," Justice Harlan predicted that the decision of the majority would "stimulate aggressions more or less brutal" upon the rights of Negroes, and would nullify the full purposes of the great Civil War amendments. Time has vindicated his argument. History has verified his prophecy.

The sanctioning of compulsory racial segregation on the railroads of Louisiana by *Plessy v. Ferguson* was immediately seized upon as a legal benediction for racism generally. The decision unleashed a horde of segregation statutes in a dozen states, covering not merely public transportation, but schools and hospitals, hotels and restaurants, parks and playgrounds, beaches and swim-

---

6. 109 U.S. 3, 27 L. Ed. 835 (1883).
7. 163 U.S. 537, 41 L. Ed. 256 (1896).
8. 347 U.S. 438 & 497, 98 L. Ed. 583 & 591 (1954).

ming pools, zoos and golf courses, and almost all public
necessities and coveniences. Not even the sacred contract
of marriage was exempt. In Louisiana, for instance, a
husband and wife living together with God's blessing,
may be sentenced to five years at hard labor, presumably
in equal but separate prisons.

It is a mistake to assume, as many still do, that compulsory segregation goes back to the origin of slavery,
or even to the abolition of slavery at the end of the Civil
War. It does not. It is primarily a twentieth-century
evil. There were few segregation statutes before *Plessy
v. Ferguson* gave the constitutional green light to racism
in 1896.[9]

The harm was not undone for two generations. Fifty-
eight years later, in the *School Segregation Cases* of
1954 and in subsequent supporting decisions, the Court
adopted the dissenting opinion of Justice Harlan, and
reversed *Plessy v. Ferguson*. As a result the supreme
law of the land now is that the "equal protection of the
laws" clause of the Fourteenth Amendment is violated
by *any* racial segregation or discrimination *accomplished
by state law or state action;* moreover, that the "due
process" clause of the Fifth Amendment is violated by
any racial segregation or discrimination *owing to federal
law or federal action.* I will not pause to delineate the
gradual change in judicial thinking which made this
reversal constitutionally inevitable, to expound the an-
nounced reasons for it, or to emphasize the Court's
humility and courage in making it.[10] Suffice it to note
that these decisions are among the greatest natural law
judgments in the history of the Court. Another formidable obstacle to human dignity, freedom, and equality,
has finally been removed. We are still advancing in wisdom and in grace.

After this long and I fear tedious background, we

---

9. Cf. Woodward, C. Vann, *The Strange Career of Jim Crow*
(1957) and Tannenbaum, Frank, *Slave and Citizen* (1947).

10. Cf. Kenealy, "Racism, Law and Politics," *supra* note 1.

come to the present-day problems of the legality and
the morality of the "freedom rides" and the various
forms of "sit-ins," "stand-ins," "wade-ins," and the like.
I confine myself, of course, to these activities in which
the participants have been orderly and peaceful, whether
or not bystanders and objectors have been unruly and
violent. To the best of my knowledge, it has been the
bystanders and objectors who have shouted the insults,
thrown the rocks, swung the tire chains, wielded the
baseball bats, fired the bombs, burned the buses, and
inflicted the personal injuries. The conduct and spirit
of the Freedom Riders and the sit-in participants are
reflected in the Negro Students Code, drawn up by Negro
students in Nashville, Tennessee:[11]

> Don't strike back or curse if abused.
> Don't laugh out.
> Don't hold conversations with floor workers.
> Don't block entrances to the stores and the aisles.
> Show yourself courteous and friendly at all times.
> Sit straight and always face the counter.
> Remember love and non-violence.
> May God bless each of you.

I do not know what it is like to sit straight and face
the counter, while a thug grinds a lighted cigarette in my
back. I do not know what it takes to be courteous and
friendly, when a hoodlum swings a hammer at my head
or throws a bomb in my bus. But I do know that the
patience, the self-control, and the sufferings of the sit-
in demonstrations and the Freedom Riders, in their de-
votion to the cause of freedom and equality, have dis-
turbed and inspired the conscience of a nation. Heroic
as their activities have been, are they legally justified?
Since there is an important constitutional difference,
involving the distribution of federal and state power, between interstate commerce and local business, I shall first
discuss the Freedom Rides and the sit-ins involving

---

11. *New York Times*, March 2, 1960.

interstate commerce. And then the more difficult problem of those involving local businesses unconnected with interstate commerce.

To escape the business jealousies and legal recriminations which were Balkanizing the original states and threatening to ruin their economies, the states ceded to the federal government the power to "regulate Commerce . . . among the several States."[12] In matters requiring a single uniform rule, federal power is exclusive, and the states may not regulate. In other matters, the states retain concurrent power; provided, of course, that in case of conflict the federal power prevails. Moreover, in order that the federal power may accomplish its constitutional purpose, it extends, not merely to business activities which intrinsically *constitute* interstate commerce, but also to those local activities which *affect* interstate commerce, and the regulation of which is necessary for the efficient regulation of interstate commerce.[13] (1914).

Now transportation is obviously commerce, and activities which affect interstate transportation are clearly within federal power. Two cases are in point.

The case of *Morgan v. Virginia* in 1946[14] involved a Virginia statute which required racial segregation on interstate buses traveling through that state. At that time Congress had not exercised its superior federal power to forbid segregation on interstate carriers. Nevertheless, the Court decided:

> As there is no federal act dealing with the separation of races in interstate transportation, we must decide the validity of this Virginia statute on the challenge that it interferes with commerce, as a matter of balance between the exercise of the local police power and the need for national uniformity in the regulations for interstate travel. It seems clear to us that seating

---

12. U. S. Const., Art. I, Sec. 8, Clause 3.
13. *The Shreveport Rate Case*, 234 U.S. 342, 58 L. Ed. 1341
14. 328 U.S. 373, 90 L. Ed. 1317 (1946).

arrangements for the different races in interstate motor travel require a single uniform rule to promote and protect national travel. Consequently, we hold the Virginia statute in controversy invalid.

This holding was enunciated eight years before the 1954 decisions which invalidated *all state discrimination* as against the "equal protection" clause of the Fourteenth Amendment, and *all federal discrimination* as against the "due process" clause of the Fifth. The invalidity of this Virginia statute was predicated upon the interstate commerce clause *alone,* and without any implementing act of Congress dealing specifically with racial discrimination. As a result of *Morgan v. Virginia,* it became unnecessary for Negroes and whites, travelling in buses from the District of Columbia to the state of Virginia, to continue their little game of musical chairs in the middle of the Memorial Bridge.

The case of *Boynton v. Virginia* in 1960[15] involved another Virginia statute and a restaurant serving passengers traveling in interstate commerce. A Negro student purchased a bus ticket from Washington, D. C., to Montgomery, Alabama. When the bus arrived at the terminal in Richmond, Virginia, for a regular forty-minute stopover, the student alighted and entered a segregated restaurant in the terminal. Disregarding the segregation, he seated himself in the "white section" and requested some tea and a sandwich. When ordered by the manager to leave that section, he refused. The local constabulary were summoned. The student was arrested, tried, convicted, and fined in the local court for violation of a state "criminal trespass" statute, by reason of his refusal to leave the premises of another after having been ordered to do so by the manager of the same.

It is significant that the restaurant was not owned or operated by the bus company, but by an independent company which had a contract as lessee of the bus com-

---

15. 364 U.S. 454 (1960).

pany. Nevertheless, the restaurant was located in the terminal, and served both interstate and intrastate customers. Moreover, the buses made regular stops at the terminal so that passengers might purchase food and refreshments.

The Court, in *Boynton v. Virginia,* decided that service in such a restaurant did *affect* interstate transportation, and therefore that it was within the power of the federal government to regulate it; that the power had been exercised, and racial discrimination in such a restaurant forbidden, by a section of the Interstate Commerce Act which provides in part:

> It shall be unlawful for any common carrier by motor vehicle engaged in interstate . . . commerce to make, give, or cause any undue or unreasonable preference or advantage to any particular person . . . in any respect whatsoever; or to subject any particular person . . . to any unjust or unreasonable prejudice or disadvantage in any respect whatsoever.

The judgment of the Court, therefore, was that that section of the Act gave the student passenger a federal right to non-discriminatory service. Hence he was not a trespasser in refusing to leave the "white section" of this privately owned and operated restaurant at the command of the manager. Consequently, the Virginia "criminal trespass" statute, however valid in other respects, was unconstitutional *as applied to him.* Unlike *Morgan v. Virginia,* the Court found it unnecessary to decide the constitutional question as to whether this statute could stand as against the commerce clause *alone,* in the absence of an act of Congress. For in *Boynton* the Court found the Interstate Commerce Act sufficient to establish the federal right which prevails, of course, over any inconsistent state statute.

Thus it seems established and certain that Freedom Rides *in* interstate transportation, and sit-ins at restaurants and other accommodations *affecting* interstate transportation, are protected by a paramount federal right with which no state statute can interfere. And this is true whether the state statute attempts to compel racial discrimination baldly and expressly, or attempts to do so by the more sophisticated devices of "criminal trespass," "disorderly conduct," or other statutes.

The problem of the Freedom Rides and the sit-ins in local businesses, unrelated to interstate commerce, is more difficult. The starting point in this problem is the Supreme Court's decision in the *Civil Rights Cases* of 1883, mentioned above. The legal difficulty is as follows.

After the ratification of the Civil War amendments, and assuming to enforce the same by appropriate legislation in accordance with the express provisions of the last sections of the Amendments, the Congress passed the Civil Rights Act of 1875, the last civil rights act for eighty-two years, before those of 1937 and 1960. The Act of 1875 provided in part:

> That all persons within the jurisdiction of the United States shall be entitled to the full and equal enjoyment of the accommodations, advantages, facilities, and privileges of inns, public conveyances on land or water, theatres, and other places of public amusement; subject only to the conditions and limitations established by law, and applicable alike to citizens of every race and color, regardless of any previous condition of servitude.

Thereafter, five separate cases, based upon alleged racial discrimination in violation of the above Act, were brought in various federal courts. The Supreme Court eventually decided all five cases in one consolidated opinion known as the *Civil Rights Cases* of 1883. Two of the cases were against owners of inns or hotels; one against Maguire's Theatre in San Francisco; one against the Grand Opera House of New York; and the other against the Memphis & Charleston Railroad.

Justice Bradley delivered the opinion of the Court which may be summarized briefly as follows. Regarding the Thirteenth Amendment, which outlawed slavery in all forms throughout the United States, the Congress is fully empowered to adopt general and direct legislation, respecting either state or private action, for the purpose of preventing slavery or the necessary incidents or badges thereof; but racial discrimination in places of public accommodation does not amount to slavery or a necessary incident or badge thereof; therefore the Act was not authorized under that Amendment. Regarding the Fourteenth Amendment, which is a limitation upon state action only, the Congress is empowered to adopt, not general and direct legislation respecting private action, but only corrective legislation respecting state discrimination; but the Act attempts to regulate, not state discrimination, but private discrimination on the part of private owners and operators of private businesses; it was not authorized, therefore, under that Amendment. The Fifteenth Amendment, concerning voting rights, was not involved. To hold otherwise would destroy the principle of federalism enshrined in the Tenth Amendment. The Act of 1875 is unconstitutional.

In the subsequent light of *Morgan v. Virginia* in 1946, and *Boynton v. Virginia* in 1960, it is interesting to note that in the *Civil Rights Cases* of 1883 an argument was made that the Act of 1875 was constitutional at least as applied to the one case involving the Memphis & Charleston Railroad, an interstate carrier. But the Court brushed aside the contention by observing that the Act of 1875 was conceived, not under the federal interstate commerce clause, but under the Civil War amendments.

Justice Harlan, whose 1896 dissent in *Plessy v. Ferguson* was eventually adopted by the Court in the 1954 *Segregation Cases,* also dissented in the 1883 *Civil Rights Cases.* In brief summary, he argued that racial discrimination in places of public accommodation was indeed a *badge of slavery,* being founded upon the very white supremacy doctrine which was at the root of slavery, and being a direct continuance of the racial degradation

which was the fruit of slavery, and hence the Act was
authorized by the Thirteenth Amendment; moreover, discrimination in places of *public accommodation,* so essential to life in organized society, was indeed discrimination *by the state itself,* which licensed and sanctioned the
policies of such establishments, and hence the Act was
authorized by the Fourteenth Amendment also. In reply
to the argument that his opinion would destroy the principle of federalism enshrined in the Tenth Amendment,
Justice Harlan was careful to point out:

> I do not contend that the Thirteenth Amendment in-
> vests Congress with authority, by legislation, to define
> and regulate the entire body of civil rights which
> citizens enjoy, or may enjoy, in the several states.
> But I hold that since slavery, as the court has repeated-
> ly declared, was the moving or principal cause of the
> adoption of that amendment, and since that institution
> rested wholly upon the inferiority, as a race, of those
> held in bondage, their freedom necessarily involved
> immunity from, and protection against all discrimi-
> nation against them, because of their race, in respect
> of such civil rights as belong to freemen of other races.

But Justice Harlan did not prevail. The Court has
not yet adopted his dissent in this case, as it has since
adopted his dissent in *Plessy v. Ferguson.* The *Civil
Rights Cases* of 1883 still hold that racial discrimination
is neither slavery nor a badge of slavery, and that the
"equal protection" clause of the Fourteenth Amendment
forbids *state action only,* not discrimination by private
persons or corporations. Is the legal situation hopeless?
Will the Court change or distinguish its position?

A few important cases may indicate a trend towards
change or distinction. In 1917, before *Plessy v. Ferguson* was overruled, the case of *Buchanan v. Warley*[16] held
invalid a Louisville, Kentucky, zoning ordinance which
effected racial segregation in housing. The invalidity

---

16. 245 U.S. 60 (1917).

was predicated however, not on "equal protection of the laws," but upon "due process of law" concerning rights in real property. Since this decision outlawed municipal ordinances and state statutes from segregating housing, various devices were concocted to accomplish the same result by *private action*.

A favorite device was, and seemingly still is, the racially restrictive covenant used to prevent sale of land to, or occupancy of land by, Negroes; and according to which Negroes who took possession of such "restricted" property became subject to suit to divest them of title and to revest it in the vendor or another of the Caucasian race. But in the extremely important case of *Shelley v. Kraemer* in 1948,[17] a unanimous Court held that, although the restrictive covenant in itself, as a private contract, did not constitute racial discrimination by the state, yet the *enforcement* of such a covenant by state courts did constitute *racial discrimination by the state* contrary to the Fourteenth Amendment. Chief Justice Vinson said for the Court:

> Since the decision of this Court in the Civil Rights Cases, 109 U.S. 3, the principle has become firmly imbedded in our constitutional law that the action inhibited by the first section of the Fourteenth Amendment is only such action as may fairly be said to be that of the states. . . . So long as the purposes of those agreements are effectuated by voluntary adherence to their terms, it would appear clear that there has been no action by the State and the provisions of the Amendment have not been violated. . . . But here there was more. These are cases in which the purposes of the agreements were secured only by judicial enforcement by state courts of the restrictive terms of the agreements.

After the Shelley case individuals who breached the racially restrictive covenants could not be enjoined from

---

17. 334 U.S. 1, 92 L. Ed. 1178 (1948).

doing so.   Nevertheless, a number of attempts were made
to sue for money damages for the breach of such covenants.   However, such attempts were also unsuccessful.
In *Barrows v. Jackson* in 1953[18] the Court held that such
suits were also impermissible, as an indirect way of en-
forcing racial discrimination *by state action*.   The covenant decisions make it clear that neither state nor federal
courts may enforce private agreements which are racially
discriminatory.

A few years before *Shelley* and *Barrows,* another case
of very great significance was decided by the Court.
Marsh v. Alabama in 1946[19] involved a town named
Chickasaw, a suburb of Mobile, Alabama, which was
wholly owned and operated — houses, streets, sewerage
system, stores and facilities — by the Gulf Shipbuilding
Corporation.   It was similar to all other nearby towns in
every important respect, except for its private ownership
and operation.   A Jehovah's Witness entered Chickasaw
for the purpose of distributing some religious literature.
She was told by the town manager that she could not do
so without a permit, and that a permit would not be
granted.   She protested and was directed to leave.   She
refused to do so and the police arrested and charged her
with a violation of Alabama's typical "criminal trespass"
statute, which provides that it is a crime to enter or
remain on private property after having been warned
not to do so.   The Court through Justice Black said:

> Our question then narrows down to this: Can those
> people who live in or come to Chickasaw be denied
> freedom of press or religion simply because a single
> company has title to all the town? . . . We do not agree
> that the corporation's property interests settle the
> question. . . . Ownership does not always mean absolute
> dominion. The more an owner, for his advantage, opens
> up his property for use by the public in general, the
> more do his rights become circumscribed by the statu-

18. 346 U.S. 249 (1953).
19. 326 U.S. 501, 90 L. Ed. 265 (1946).

tory and constitutional rights of those who use it. . . .
When we balance the constitutional rights of owners
of property against those of the people to enjoy freedom of press and religion, as we must here, we remain
mindful of the fact that the latter occupy a preferred
position. . . . In so far as the State has attempted to
impose criminal punishment on appellant for undertaking to distribute religious literature in a company
town, its action cannot stand.

Justice Frankfurter, in a concurring opinion, re-
marked: "And similarly the technical distinctions on
which a finding of 'trespass' so often depends are too
tenuous to control decision regarding the scope of the
vital liberties guaranteed by the Constitution." It is
clear that the owner of the company town cannot make
use of state criminal law to vindicate his alleged "property right." This being so, it seems to me that the owner
is not entitled to "self-help" either. In a word, the appellant had a federal right to distribute her religious
literature, in peaceable and orderly fashion, in reasonable
and timely manner, on this privately owned and operated
property, even against the express wishes of the owner,
and against the express provisions of state law. I readily concede that the application of *Marsh v. Alabama* and
Shelley v. Kraemer to the intrastate sit-ins is not without
difficulty. The cases are distinguishable on the facts.
But it seems to me that the distinction is one of degree
only.

Three most interesting intrastate sit-in cases are
scheduled for argument in the October, 1961, term of the
United States Supreme Court. All three cases arose out
of Baton Rouge, Louisiana, and were decided adversely
to the participants by the Supreme Court of that state
on October 5, 1960. On March 20, 1961, petitions for
writs of certiorari to that state court were granted, and
the cases were ordered to be consolidated for argument
the following fall. The cases are *Mary Briscoe et al. v.
Louisiana, John Garner et al. v. Louisiana,* and *Jannette
Hoston et al. v. Louisiana.* The Briscoe group sat-in at

the lunch counter of the Greyhound Bus Station on March 29, 1960. The Garner group sat-in at the lunch counter of Sitman's Drug Store the same day. The Hoston group beat them to it by sitting-in at the lunch counter of S. H. Kress & Company, a large department store, on the previous day, March 28, 1960. One intriguing feature of the cases is that the arresting officer in all three cases was Captain Weiner of the Baton Rouge City Police, whose testimony of what actually happened may turn out to be the best break the sit-ins have ever had in the South.

It appears from the Brief for the Petitioners, which is the only account I have seen of the case, that all three establishments are open to the general public and serve all members of the public without discrimination, except at the lunch counter — the high altar of white supremacy. The three groups of sit-ins seated themselves sacrilegiously at the lunch counters and requested service in an orderly and peaceable fashion. Consternation reigned among the white hierarchy. Service was refused, either in observance of personal prejudice or in deference to community pressure and in the interests of free enterprise.

In the case of the Briscoe group at the Greyhound Bus Station, it would appear that the waitress did not demand that the sitters leave, although the evidence on that point is slightly conflicting. But in the cases of the Garner group at Sitman's Drug Store, and of the Hoston group at Kress' Department Store, it seems quite clear that, although the participants were denied service, they were not ordered or requested to leave by anyone speaking for the management. In the Briscoe case, the police were summoned by an anonymous telephone call; in the Garner case, by the officer on the beat who observed the strange goings-on; and in the Hoston case, by the manager of the store who, however, merely advised the police that the participants were seated at counters reserved for whites. It would appear that in all three cases, with the dubious exception of the Briscoe case, the only persons who objected to the participants' presence and who requested them to leave were the anonymous telephoner and the *police*. And it would appear that, only upon refusal to leave at *police* request, the participants were arrested for violation of the Louisiana statute against "disturbing the peace." For this evidence the petitioners are indebted to the testimony of the arresting officer, Captain Weiner. The Louisiana statute prohibiting "disturbing the peace" reads in pertinent part:

Disturbing the peace is the doing of any of the following in such a manner as would foreseeably disturb or alarm the public:

(5) Holding an unlawful assembly; or

(7) Commission of any other act in such a manner as to unreasonably disturb or alarm the public.

I have omitted (1) fist fights, (2) insulting language, (3) intoxication, (4) violent and tumultuous conduct by three of more persons, and (6) the interruption of a lawful assembly of people. None of these specifications were pertinent. As to (5), an unlawful assembly, its only pertinence would obviously run afoul of the Fourteenth Amendment, because the state cannot make an integrated assembly unlawful. As to (7) — any other act unreasonably disturbing or alarming to the public — I assume that it is settled that an integrated luncheon could not possibly be *reasonably* alarming or disturbing to a civilized public, at least in 1960.

Wherefore, I am convinced that these Louisiana convictions will be reversed because (1) there was most obviously no "disturbance of the peace," which was the alleged crime; because (2) there was not even the infringement of an alleged "property right," since, with the very dubious exception of the Briscoe group, no owner or authorized representative of a private owner requested the participants to leave the premises; and because (3) the police action which was the sum and substance of

the whole proceedings was quite obviously *state action,*
to enforce a *state policy* of racial segregation in defiance
of the Fourteenth Amendment and the decrees of the
United States Supreme Court.   Not merely from personal
experience, but from the abundant public record, I
assume that the last reason needs no documentation for
any student of interracial history.

It is at least temerarious to predict future decisions
of the Supreme Court in the difficult area of possible
reversals of judgments, distinctions in interpretation,
changes in judicial policy, and advances in the political
philosophy of freedom and equality.   History testifies
to this. Nevertheless, I am rash enough to hope that the
Court will reverse the convictions of the three sit-in
groups from Louisiana.   On the whole facts, their convictions seem to be based upon *state action* and determination to enforce *state policy* of racial discrimination.

However, if the Court reverses the convictions, but
does so on the narrow ground that it was not the pro-
prietors, but the police, who made the formal and technical requests to leave the premises, and *therefore* the discrimination was state action, then I would consider the
reversals a shallow victory for interracial justice.   The
result would simply be that, in future cases, the pro-
prietors or their servants would simply make sure to
make a formal and technical order for the sitters to leave
the premises, and to make sure that the police do not
anticipate or pre-empt the technical formality in their
zeal to enforce and preserve the *officially determined*
state *"way of life."*

There is wisdom in Justice Frankfurter's concurring
observation in the case of *Marsh v. Alabama:* ". . . the
technical distinctions on which a finding of 'trespass' so
often depends are too tenuous to control decision regarding the scope of the vital liberties guaranteed by the
Constitution."   This is true, not merely of trespass, but
of disturbance of the peace, disorderly conduct, and similar technical or vague charges.   It would be a tragic

shame, it seems to me, if fundamental rights of human dignity and equality should become dependent upon purely formal and technical declarations of so-called property rights in businesses which, although privately owned, are nevertheless voluntarily dedicated to, and dependent for profits upon, the *public interest* and the *public accommodation*. It seems to me that our Federal Constitution is directed to more substantial objectives and purposes.

Suppose, however, that constitutional law doctrine does not develop to embrace Justice Harlan's *Civil Rights* dissent (as it did develop to embrace his *Plessy* dissent). Suppose that the Supreme Court declines to invalidate the state convictions of local sit-ins based upon "criminal trespass," "disturbance of peace," "disorderly conduct," and similar statutes. What conclusion should be drawn? Most certainly *not* that the Federal Constitution or the Supreme Court approves or sanctions such clearly immoral and un-Christian racism. But *merely* that the Federal Constitution, as presently interpreted by the Supreme Court, and as the charter of a federal government of limited powers, is unable to afford a *remedy* for the grave evil. The only solution, therefore, would be in a new federal amendment to provide a federal remedy, the enactment of civil rights legislation in the states, or the public pressure of more sit-ins.

It should be noted that some twenty-seven states, comprising a substantial majority of Americans, have civil-rights legislation making racial discrimination in places and businesses of public accommodation, privately owned or not, a criminal offense. This is heartening corroboration of the natural law and of Christian doctrine. But, in the absence of federal power, what about the encouragement, toleration, or permission of some local states *in re* racism in public accommodations. Are the sit-ins morally justified? It seems to me that they are.

Assuming as before that they are orderly and peace-

ful, they appear to be the only practical way to induce
a moral and Christian practice into an important aspect
of public life. The motive is exemplary: to arouse the
conscience of the community in favor of justice and
equality. The circumstances seem propitious: the failure of other means, the frustration of purely legal victories, the inspiration to the weak and the frightened,
and the signal success in many cities. The conduct itself is peaceful and orderly. The enormity of the moral
evil to be overcome is apparent: the widespread denial
of fundamental human dignity, freedom, and equality,
the consequent moral evils both in the individual persons
(persecuted and persecutors) and in the civil community.

No moral rights of private property are transgressed.
No man has a moral right to use his property, a creature
of God, against the children of God. Racial discrimination, even in the use of purely private property, is immoral at least as transgressing the supreme law of
charity. The sit-ins, however, are not concerned with
purely private property, or with securing the observance
of charity in private homes, private clubs, private activities. Their concern is with justice in public life, public
businesses, and public accommodations. They are entitled to seek that end by peaceable, orderly, and by
public means. Their dedication to such a cause is not
a violation or defiance of any just law — and only a just
law can bind the human conscience. The public welfare
and the peace of the nation will benefit from the inspir-
ing self-sacrifice of the participants in the sit-ins. The
law itself will be purified by their efforts. The cause of
justice will be served. The country will be better off for
those brave youths, Negro and white, who have seen
the vision of a better future and who have the heart to
pursue it.

THOMAS P. MELADY
is President of Consul-
tants for Overseas Relations,
Inc. Author of the recently published,
Profiles of African Leaders, *Dr. Melady was*
formerly economic advisor to the Ethiopian government
and is Chairman of the Africa Committee of the Catholic
Association for International Peace. He is founder of the
Institute of African Affairs at Duquesne University
and is a director of various organiza-
tions active in international affairs
and in Africa.

AFRICAN INDEPENDENCE
AND THE NEGRO PEOPLES

The rise and spread of nationalism throughout the world which followed in the wake of the second World War, set into motion a concatenation of events the consequences of which had far-reaching implications for international relations.

Nowhere else was the impact of the new nationalism felt as strongly as in Africa, where it kindled a fire which within a remarkably short time has swept across that continent, altering irrevocably social, political, and economic landscapes, obliterating empires once thought impregnable, and giving voice to peoples who for generations have stood silent.

Nationalism has proved itself an enduring force, and it is not likely that either its appeal or its dynamism will be appreciably mitigated in the foreseeable future. Opinion formerly held that once primary aims such as independence and sovereignty had been achieved, nationalism, having won its battles, would have no further enemy to vanquish. This opinion is little entertained today. With increasing clarity, it has become apparent that the achievement of primary objectives can serve as easily to re-enforce nationalist proclivities as to abate them.

What was the origin of this nationalism which today commands so powerful a force in Africa? It did not derive from a single cause but rather was the result of a multiplicity of factors, each of which contributed to its

birth and development. Much of its early impetus de-
rived from American influence; initially from the attention focused on the problems facing the Negro in the
aftermath of the Civil War, but later from the pens of
such writers as W. E. B. Du Bois and George Padmore,
or by efforts such as the Garvey Movement which sought
to promote a "back-to-Africa" drive among American
Negroes. Aimé Cesaire, West Indian poet and member
of the French Parliament, added the concept of the
personalité africaine, and was among the first who sought
to reclaim Africa's cultural heritage and to assert the
individuality of the Negro peoples.

The iniquities suffered by the Negro, and the concern
to which these gave rise, served as a natural springboard
from which sympathy was later transferred to other
underprivileged peoples. As the Negro began to gain an
identity for himself and to demand increasingly his rights
as a citizen, what had begun as little more than a community of outcasts gradually began to develop into a socially conscious group, aware for the first time that the
Negro of Africa and the Negro of the New World pos-
sessed a common cultural heritage and shared certain
interests and values. It was then that the first feelings
of kinship were felt, that the first gropings toward some
sort of unity were attempted, and that Pan-African
nationalism was born.

Although nationalism differs in character according
to the specific historic conditions and the peculiar social structure of each country, in Africa, its development
has been remarkably uniform owing to the similarity of
social, cultural, and political factors and to the common
experience under colonialism which the various African
nations shared.

For the West, the nationalist revolution in postwar
Africa represents an as yet undetermined fate, the nature of which will be decided by the actions taken in
the next few years. Handicapped by its colonial background, the West enters into a contest for the loyalty
and friendship of the African peoples against a power-

ful adversary; one whose actions to date have shown him adept at persuading the newly independent peoples of Africa that his philosophy and form of political organization is superior to ours for helping them to solve the problems with which they are confronted.

The problem of establishing rapport and mutual trust with the peoples of newly independent but still economically underdeveloped countries is not solely a political one. It has its social and moral aspects as well. The contest which today is being waged in Africa between East and West has implications which go far beyond the borders of the territories concerned. Africa today is engaged in nothing less than a full-scale social revolution, the consequences of which will have an important bearing on the outcome of the Cold War and the power relationship between the United States and the Soviet Union. Given the present polarized state of the world and the almost daily increase in international tensions, the delicate balance of power now more or less existent between East and West can only be decisively increased or decreased in terms of the sympathy and support gained from the new states. No longer taken for granted as they once were, nations belonging neither to one camp nor to the other and committed neither to Western democracy nor Eastern communism but boasting their own unique conceptions of political philosophy, have come into their own as important powers in the international scene. The reality of this so-called "third force," often referred to as the neutralist bloc, began with the historic conference at Bandung in 1955, and has continued to consolidate its position and to increase its action since that time. Many of the newly independent African states, whether by conviction or by fear, have been prompted to align themselves with this third group rather than commit themselves unreservedly to either the Soviet Union or to the United States.

As a cohesive political bloc, the new nations of Africa can be expected to play an increasingly important role in the councils of the world and in the direction of international relations. Numbering at present twenty-nine, they have already shown themselves capable of wielding an important influence on matters of international concern, as the U.N. votes on Angola have forcefully proved. With the support of an important number of the Asian nations also of neutralist persuasion, the so-called Afro-Asian bloc has emerged as the singularly most powerful group in the world body today.

The rapid rise and spread of nationalism in Africa following the end of World War II was the result of the introduction of numerous outside influences into that continent which acted as catalysts activating latent sentiments of anti-colonialism long dormant among the indigenous peoples. The liberal principles expressed in such doctrines as the Atlantic Charter and, subsequently, in the Charter of the United Nations in 1945, as well as the frequently expressed anti-colonial policies evinced by certain wartime leaders, did much to awaken among the peoples of underdeveloped areas a consciousness of their subordinate status and to incite among them a spirit of revolt against those who in their eyes were their oppressors. The extraordinary amount of publicity which accompanied the announcement of the programs and ideals of the then newly created United Nations — much of which found its way into areas still under colonial rule — did much to excite public imagination and to foster in such areas the conviction that, with time, independence would be a thing within the reach of all.

To the attention devoted to the activities of the U.N. was also added the fact that British territories in Africa were promised self-rule as a matter of principle, if not in the immediate future, then at least at a proximate date when it was felt internal conditions within the various territories would be such as to permit a peaceable transfer of authority to competent African officials.

In French Africa, the significance of these developments did not go unnoticed. The inflation and shortage of consumer goods which plagued French Africa all during the years of the war as a result of its separation from France, continued well after hostilities had been ended. This, added to the traumatic experience of life under Vichy-dominated colonial administrations, came to represent, in the eyes of many, the worst and most oppressive aspects of colonialism.

African nationalism, however, received its real stimulus with the independence of the Gold Coast in 1957. Although other African states such as Ethiopia and Liberia possess a long tradition of independence and sovereignty antedating that of the Gold Coast, which adopted the name of the ancient African kingdom of Ghana, it was the latter which more than any other excited the imagination of an Africa still overwhelmingly under colonial domination and which came to symbolize the hopes of its eventual total independence.

It would be difficult to exaggerate the impact of Ghanaian independence on African nationalism. What rendered it a thing of such force was the fact that its realization represented the establishment of the first truly progressive voice in Africa; one which henceforth could be expected to speak on behalf of those of its brethren peoples still under colonial rule. It was as if each African had had a personal stake in the young nation's fate. Its success would prove beyond question that Africans were capable of ruling themselves and of solving their own problems; its failure would only serve to re-enforce the often repeated claims of some European elements that Africans were but children in need of guidance from the outside.

With the achievement of Ghanaian independence, nationalism everywhere in Africa received a powerful impetus. Fledgling nationalist groups, only half-hopeful at first of succeeding in their efforts at freeing their countries from colonial rule, drew new strength and encouragement from the creation of the new nation. Hundreds at first, then thousands, and finally millions, started to take up the cry for freedom and independence. Tribal and ethnic differences and traditional rivalries began to be overlooked or even forgotten as Africans began to realize that only through joining their efforts and consolidating their ranks could they hope to wrest concessions from a reluctant colonial world.

As the fire of independence which had been ignited in Ghana began to spread across the face of Africa, the reactions on the part of the various colonial powers which still controlled much of the continent differed markedly. Adamant at first, some gradually came around to realizing the deeper implications of the nationalist ferment and began to institute far-reaching, if long-overdue, reforms, partly out of genuine concern and liberal conviction, but partly, too, out of fear that, unless something were done quickly, what had started as a spark might develop into a conflagration soon to be beyond their control. Others, determined to maintain their hold on their African possessions, merely dug themselves in deeper and proceeded to put into operation even more stringent measures designed to keep the autochthonous peoples under control. Great Britain and France were notable subjects of the former reaction; Portugal and South Africa, notorious examples of the latter. Somewhere in between lay the Spanish and the Belgians; the former with but relatively insignificant holdings in Africa, the latter still masters of the vastly rich and important Congo.

The issue was not exclusively one of nationalism versus colonialism; it was much more complex. It represented not merely a choice of one or the other of these alternatives, but rather involved a searching re-examination of the fundamental moral, social, and political beliefs by which men had lived for generations and in conformity with which nations had molded official policies of colonial rule. Once cherished beliefs and time-honored formulas of colonial administration underwent profound scrutiny as rapidly moving events and increased militancy on the part of African nationalist leaders, as well as an awakening consciousness among the African masses, proved these beliefs inadequate or inapplicable in the light of changing political situations.

In British territories, eventual independence for all African territories became an accepted matter of policy, while in French Africa the much heralded policy of assimilation gave way first to one of "association," then to one of "independence within interdependence," and finally to one which acknowledged that complete autonomy was inevitable.

The granting of independence to French and British colonies in Africa has had far-reaching repercussions not merely throughout the rest of Africa, where it has effected a profound change in the relations between Europeans and their former subject peoples, but in the United Nations as well, where the presence of the new African states has created a new power bloc which, in time, may well come to be the most important in the world body.

In 1960, the majority of African states gained their independence. The impact of this fact on the United Nations has been that the balance of power in the proceedings of the General Assembly is now within momentary grasp of the Afro-Asian states. These states are now equal partners with the West, not only in the United Nations, but in other international organizations as well. The determination of these new countries to exercise their proper role in international problems was perhaps best summed up by Ismael Touré, brother of President Sekou Touré of Guinea, when, at the Afro-Asian Conference held in Conakry in April, 1960, he stated: "Conscious of our numbers, our economic and cultural potentialities, strong in faith and moral resources, we can on the one condition of unity and solidarity, play forthwith a decisive part in the solution of all political, social and diplomatic problems of the world."

Forty-nine nations at the United Nations represent the non-Western world. These states, coupled with the seventeen Latin American states, give the non-Anglo-Saxon oriented cultures a clear majority in U.N. proceedings. Indicative of their accelerated strength, the new and older African and Asian countries now have forty-nine votes in the General Assembly of the United Nations,

out of a total of one hundred and three. When these
political facts are added to the economic reality of the
growing dependence of the Western industrial nations on
the Afro-Asian states for their raw materials and for
markets for their finished products, the good political
reasons for the West's interest in the newly emerging
nations become apparent.

The phenomenon of the emergent political presence
of the non-white peoples in the world today inevitably
relates itself to the current status of the American Negro.
What are the implications of the dramatic "coming to
power" of the non-white peoples? For the United States,
these implications are directly related to the role of our
country in protecting its best interests. The United States
must win the good will and trust of the non-white peoples, especially those in Africa, if it is to maintain its
independence in face of the threat presented by the
Sino-Soviet entente, dedicated to its destruction.

There is increasing concern in the highest echelons
of our society that we are not winning — and perhaps
are losing — the good will of the African and Asian
peoples. This concern has caused our leaders in government, industry, education, and religion to re-examine
carefully the causes of this condition so that effective
remedial action may be undertaken.

In the myraid of problems which confront Africa, race
looms as one of the most important as well as one of
the most complex. Unlike what is so often believed, the
race question does not express itself solely in terms of
blatant Negro-white conflict as represented by the situation existing in South Africa or the Portuguese colonies.
Within African societies themselves, there are numerous
mutually antagonistic elements emanating from deep-
seated hostilities and quarrels of long standing. Ethnic
division, often vociferously expressed, confronts African
sovereignty with one of its most serious problems and
stands as an obstacle to the achievement of one of the
major African goals, namely, the creation of a national
consciousness.

The question of race must of necessity be included in any discussion concerned with African-American relations. Its immediacy arises in part from the as yet unsettled state of Negro-white relations in the United States and the impact which their progress or regression inevitably creates abroad.

One of the primary causes for the increasing antipathy with which the United States is being regarded by many Afro-Asian peoples stems from the discriminatory treatment accorded the Negro in our own society. African and Asian visitors have widely observed the differences in status between white and Negro citizens in this country. Some, as the recent case of Dr. William Fitzjohn, diplomat from Sierra Leone, illustrated, have themselves been the victims of racial discrimination, a practice endured daily by an important portion of our own citizenry. Such occurrences, coupled with the extensive publicity given abroad to such incidents as took place in Little Rock, New Orleans, and Birmingham, cannot but create in the minds of the Afro-Asian peoples the certitude that the United States is in fact little better than the Union of South Africa where the treatment of its non-white population is concerned.

Africans and Asians obviously resent such discriminations which seem deliberately directed against people of color in a country whose Constitution proclaims equality and justice for all. Nor should it be forgotten that few of them will feel inspired to speak in defense of a nation whose moral and political philosophy proclaim one set of values but whose daily social practices bespeak another.

The inconsistency between theory and practice in matters of racial tolerance as evidenced in the United States may be rationalized by some as but one of the ineluctable results, if not attributes, of a genuinely democratic system in which pluralism of beliefs and of differing social systems is an integral part. Few people, however, may be expected to entertain so academic a view. For the vast majority of Africans and Asians as well as for the American Negro, racial prejudice, discrimination, and intolerance, represent something far more real and immediate than merely another subject for after-dinner discussion. The impact of the reality of this problem and the extent of its immediacy is more readily appreciated when one becomes aware of the tensions to which it gives rise in present-day American society. The sit-in demonstrations of Nashville and the freedom rides through Alabama were, it is true, campaigns of civil disobedience; they were also, however, protests against a social injustice which neither government nor society displayed any particular hurry to correct.

The dilemma presented by the inconsistency of moral principles with social practice is not something restricted solely to the formal laws of government; it is no less grave in the field of religion, where too often in the past, moral principles have given way to administrative pressure or to political expediency rather than held their ground against patent injustice. For the Catholic Church, the problem of racial intolerance, particularly as it manifests itself in Africa, presents what is at once one of the greatest challenges to the Church and one of its most delicate tasks. In a part of the world where it has too long confined its activities largely to ministering to the spiritual needs of but a relatively small minority of whites, to the general neglect of the masses of the indigenous populations, its task must of necessity be one of expanding the base from which to recruit new members. Further, no less than other institutions which wish to function effectively and successfully in the African environment, it must plan and execute a program designed to augment the number of native clergy operative in the local area. In other words, it must pursue and encourage a deliberate policy of "Africanizing" its ranks and accord positions of responsibility and authority to Africans who so merit them. In this respect, the elevation of Bishop Rugumbwa of Tanganyika to Cardinal was an encouraging step. Other similar appointments would go a long way toward creating a more favorable image

of the Church in the eyes of the African masses whom it
would seek to have as its faithful and would aid in meeting
the stringent competition presented by Islam, a faith
which has made impressive headway in Africa precisely because of its readiness and willingness to embrace
all within its fold, irrespective of racial or cultural
affiliation.

More basic still, the Church must definitively divorce
itself, at least in matters of social policy, from exclusively metropolitan European influences and seek to establish
greater rapport with and understanding of the legitimate
aspirations of the African peoples with whom it deals.
No greater damage can be done to the mission of Christianity in Africa than to continue, whether by deliberate
intention or by noncommittal default, the promulgation
of a patent hypocrisy which preaches Christian brother-
hood on the one hand, but tolerates and supports, either
actively or tacitly, intolerant and discriminatory practices
on the other. Such a policy will only serve to discredit
the Church and its leaders in the eyes of the indigenous
peoples and render its task of proselytizing infinitely more
difficult.

The gravity of this particular problem has not everywhere been the same in Africa. In certain territories
ruled by nations possessing a traditional separation of
Church and State (as in the former French colonies for
example), the problem has been less vexing. In others,
however, where Catholicism is the officially sanctioned
religion of the State, it has inevitably been made to
share in the approbation or the condemnation which the
State has necessarily incurred from the local populace
as a result of its official policies. Portugal is the nation
which most immediately comes to mind in the latter case.
In the Portuguese colonies in Africa, notably in Angola,
Mozambique, and Portuguese Guinea, the Church has
traditionally been a silent but powerful partner of the
government, both through its control of the educational
systems of these territories and through its tacit ac-

quiescence in the colonial policy of the Portuguese government.

Recently, for reasons still not entirely known, the Church in Angola has shown far more independence of spirit than it has heretofore exhibited, and in a pastoral letter issued by the Roman Catholic bishops of Angola, went on record as urging the inhabitants of the territory to stand together for the common good: "Disillusioned people fighting against privation are a prey to despair and more apt to be carried away by dangerous ideologies and promises which cannot be fulfilled. Poverty is a bad counsellor and a threat to tranquility and peace. The solution of certain problems can be found only through united and adequate legislation and the total and generous cooperation of individuals and organizations."

Efforts such as those represented by the pastoral letter of the Roman Catholic bishops of Angola may contribute significantly to awakening metropolitan opinion to the reasons behind the current social unrest expressing itself in Angola, but it is doubtful whether they can exert anything more than an ephemeral influence in that restless territory, given the continuance of the present policies on the part of the Portuguese government. Driven by pent-up frustration which is the result of long years of life under an oppressive colonial regime, plagued with disorders inflicted by years of a harsh and unenlightened colonial policy which instituted forced labor and denied adequate representation to indigenous elements, Angola, as the rest of Portuguese Africa, suffers from a cancer which cannot and will not be cured save by major surgery.

Juridically tied to Portugal as an "overseas province," Angola is, in theory, an integral part of Portugal, as much as part of its soil as Beira or Alentojo. In reality, it was never a part of Portugal any more than Algeria was ever really a part of France. Whereas the French at last are showing signs of acknowledging and accepting the reality of their particular situation, the Portuguese have thus far demonstrated little inclination to follow their example.

The recent outbreak of violence against Portuguese settlers in Angola has been met with measures of extraordinary repression on the part of the Portuguese authorities rather than with a genuine desire to redress legitimate grievances. Clinging to her argument that she is carrying on a civilizing mission in Africa, Portugal has obdurately continued to disregard the counsels of moderation proffered by her friends, and to defy world opinion as expressed through the U.N. resolutions calling upon her to desist at once from executing further repressive measures against the Angolan populace and urging her to institute long overdue social reforms in her African territories.

Portugal's unwillingness to modify her African policies, or even to acknowledge the most remote legitimacy of the African claims made against her, poses a serious dilemma for those who have traditionally been her friends and allies. In its broadest context, her obstinacy in this regard is costing her dearly in terms of American public support. Both officially and unofficially, there is a growing consensus in the United States which appears prepared to accept whatever risks may be involved in losing Portugal's friendship, owing to a firm and unequivocal declaration of respect for human rights and adherence to the policy of self-determination for all peoples. Increasingly isolated from international public opinion, Portugal may soon find that even her often played trump card of membership in NATO is poor insurance against the criticism and pressure of world condemnation.

For Catholicism, Portuguese intransigence poses its own problem, one likely to compromise seriously the Church's effectiveness in other parts of Africa unless speedily resolved: namely, the continued association in the minds of the African masses of colonial oppression and religious acquiescence. As the situation in Angola becomes still graver and the Portuguese community (which is also the Catholic community of the country) feels itself increasingly menaced by nationalist forces and, being menaced, draws itself more closely together in self-defense, it is only reasonable to expect that Africans will perceive that those whom they conceive to be their oppressors also happen to be the stalwarts, the pillars, of a Church which speaks of brotherly love and the equality of all men before the eyes of God, but which apparently does relatively little to encourage the application of such noble principles to real life.

The unwillingness of the Church to speak out against the excesses of colonial rule or actively to support just causes aimed at ameliorating the living and working conditions of the native populace, has deprived it of what might have been its most signal victory in Portuguese Africa: namely, its ability to act as spokesman for people who had no one to speak in their behalf. Had the Portuguese clergy in Africa themselves raised the outcry against the iniquities inflicted on the African populace which today expresses its protest in the form of violence and bloody rebellion, much of the tragedy presently being witnessed in Angola, and perhaps to be witnessed yet elsewhere in the Portuguese colonies of Africa in the near future, might have been avoided. Where Catholicism might have achieved some of its most impressive gains, it has by default consigned itself to regrettable isolation among the people it sought to serve. Those questioning this view need only consider the far more impressive success enjoyed by Protestant missions in Angola as a result of their outspoken and courageous defense of native interests.

The problem which faces the Church in Angola is the same which confronts it in many other parts of Africa still under colonial influence. If it is to survive and prosper in Africa, the Church cannot remain indifferent to the problems of the colonized peoples or mute to their cries of desperation. To many Africans, Christianity and colonialism symbolize antithetical concepts of man's relation to his fellow man. The one is dedicated to brotherly love and Christian charity, the other to the exploitation of the weak and the helpless by the strong and the powerful. In view of the misfortune that too often in the past Christianity has accompanied — indeed, been an integral part — of colonial rule, it would be hopeless delusion to expect African Christians to retain for much longer firm confidence in their faith in the absence of positive action showing that the two are, in fact, not the same.

Nor can it be expected any longer, as in the past, that Africans or any other peoples of underdeveloped areas for that matter, will unquestioningly resign themselves to our indifference to their sufferings and our hostility to their nationalist aspirations on the unconvincing grounds that the latter are but expressions of communist agitation seeking to disrupt the stability of the social order. The unfortunate tendency on the part of too many persons in the West to confuse nationalism with communism and to react with as much vehemence toward the former as toward the latter has already cost the West dearly and alienated many who might otherwise have been within its ranks. Those Africans who have identified with nationalist movements have in many past instances been rejected by the Christian community as communists, without due regard ever having been given for the substance of causes they espoused, or for the sincerity of their views. Isolated from the Christian community to which many of them would have otherwise turned by nature, many found themselves with but one alternative left, namely, to become in fact the very thing they had been falsely accused of being.

In its broadest context, the problem which faces the Church is quite clear. Africans cannot and must not be expected to live as strangers in their own countries. To the extent that the Church tacitly supports or unwillingly acquiesces in the perpetuation of such a situation, its position vis-a-vis the African peoples will be increasingly compromised, and in the long run will become untenable. The issues are clearly joined. If Christianity is to survive in Africa, it must reverse its traditional role of being an adjunct of colonial rule and must put itself squarely behind legitimate nationalist movements which everywhere in Africa today are crying for social reform. To ignore this reality would be to fail to read the handwriting on the wall and to court inevitable disaster.

In light of what has been said thus far, what can be done? Is the situation too late for saving? If not, what practical measures should we encourage and actively undertake, to remedy what has already become a highly charged situation, dangerously close to explosion? In the first place, it is the view of this writer that despite the present state of events, much can still be done to arrest the deterioration of the situation and perhaps even succeed in reversing the anti-Western trend currently evident in present-day relations with Africa. The obligation of the Church to dissociate itself from purely colonial influences and to put the full weight of its support behind legitimate movements for social reform has already been mentioned. One further measure along these lines might be to encourage the formation in the newly independent African states of liberal, reform-minded Catholic youth groups and local labor unions. In this sphere, particular attention ought to be devoted to cultivating the support of student groups and outstanding intellectuals; in Africa, such groups and individuals are always articulate and important elements of the social system.

On a more general level, encouragement ought to be given to promoting extensive contacts between Africans and Americans, particularly at those levels where a genuine exchange of ideas may occur and where there is some hope of effecting a positive impression on a potential African elite. Extensive use ought to be made of American Negroes in undertaking governmental and private contacts with Africans, but race ought not be made the sole factor determining such appointments. Moreover, Negroes ought to be assigned to posts of importance in all-white areas as well as in Africa. Such a move would contribute considerably to removing African suspicions that the U.S. assigns Negroes to Africa merely because it hopes to gain greater concessions from African leaders thereby.

On a local level, militant efforts must be continued to eliminate racial discrimination in our own country and to promote integration of the American Negro into all institutions of American life. Extensive efforts must be undertaken both by the federal government as well as by local authorities to educate the American public as to the problems of the underdeveloped nations as well as to acquaint them with the cultural contributions of those nations. Every effort must be made to bring to the attention of the American people the fact that in the world of today, our own destiny as a nation is intimately bound up with that of the other peoples on the globe, all of whom have aspirations of their own for a better life for themselves and for their children.

Lastly, if we hope to gain the lasting friendship and trust of the peoples of Africa, we must never lose sight of the fact that our principal battle there, as in other areas, is not against communism, but rather against poverty, disease, injustice, and exploitation — the factors which render a society vulnerable to communism. What this means, in the last analysis, is that we must not turn our heads away from the realities of protest that nationalism expresses, but face squarely the issues and the challenges raised by that protest.

Far-reaching changes are today in the wind for all of Africa — for Algeria, Angola, Mozambique, Portuguese Guinea, South Africa, Nyasaland, the Rhodesias, Kenya, Ruanda-Urundi, and the Congo, to mention but a few areas. Unless we are prepared to cope with these areas we will find ourselves hopelessly isolated from the majority of the world's population, most of which still belongs to the camp of the have-nots. We are presently faced with what will probably be our last real chance to exert a positive moral influence on the development of these new nations in terms of the example we ourselves set, as well as in terms of the understanding and the aid which we can impart to them. To be remiss in such an opportunity would be more than mere misfortune; it would be an irremediable tragedy.

This symposium originated as a broadcast from radio station **WBAI-FM** *in New York City and was first printed in the summer, 1961, issue of* Cross Currents. *The participants are Nat Hentoff, the moderator, a former editor of* Downbeat *and a writer on folk art; James Baldwin, novelist and essayist, author of* Nobody Knows My Name *(Dial),* Go Tell It on the Mountain *(Universal),* Notes of a Native Son *(Beacon); Alfred Kazin, literary critic, author of* On Native Ground *(Anchor),* A Walker in the City *(Grove); Lorraine Hansberry, playwright, author of* A Raisin in the Sun; *Emile Capouya, an editor at Macmillan Co.; and Langston Hughes, poet and columnist for the* Chicago Defender, *author of* Simple Stakes a Claim *(Rinehart),* Selected Poems *(Knopf),* A Langston Hughes Reader *(Braziller).*

THE NEGRO

IN AMERICAN CULTURE

HENTOFF: To begin the subject, which sounds rather alarmingly vague, I'd like to start with the end of the book review that James Baldwin wrote for *The New York Times* a couple of years ago. The review was of poems of Langston Hughes, and you concluded by saying that "he is not the first American Negro to find the war between his social and artistic responsibilities all but irreconcilable."

To what extent do you find this true in your own writing in terms of the self-consciousness of being a Negro and a writer, the polarity, if it exists?

BALDWIN: Well, the first difficulty is really so simple that it's usually overlooked: to be a Negro in this country and to be relatively conscious, is to be in a rage almost all the time. So that the first problem is how to control that rage so that it won't destroy you. Part of the rage is this: it isn't only what is happening to you, but it's what's happening all around you all of the time, in the face of the most extraordinary and criminal indifference, the indifference and ignorance of most white people in this country.

Now, since this so, it's a great temptation to simplify the issues under the illusion that if you simplify them enough, people will recognize them; and this illusion is very dangerous because that isn't the way it works.

You have to decide that you can't spend the rest of your life cursing out everybody that gets in your way.

As a writer, you have to decide that what is really important is not that the people you write about are Negroes, but that they are people, and that the suffering of any person is really universal. If you can ever reach this level, if you can create a person and make other people feel what this person feels, then it seems to me that you've gone much further, not only artistically, but socially, than in the ordinary, old-fashioned protest way.

I talked about Langston not being the first poet to find these responsibilities all but irreconcilable. And he won't be the last, because it also demands a great deal of time to write, it demands a great deal of stepping out of a social situation in order to deal with it. And all the time you're out of it you can't help feeling a little guilty that you are not, as it were, on the firing line, tearing down the slums and doing all these obviously needed things, which in fact, other people can do better than you because it is still terribly true that a writer is extremely rare.

HENTOFF: Miss Hansberry, in writing *A Raisin in the Sun,* to what extent did you feel a double role, both as a kind of social actionist "protester," and as a dramatist?

MISS HANSBERRY: Well, given the Negro writer, we are necessarily aware of a special situation in the American setting. And that probably works two ways. One of them makes us sometimes forget that there is really a very limited expression in literature which is not protest, be it black, white or what have you; I can't imagine a contemporary writer any place in the world today who isn't in conflict with his world. Personally, I can't imagine a time in the world when the artist wasn't in conflict; if he was any kind of an artist, he had to be.

We are doubly aware of conflict, because of the special pressures of being a Negro in America, but I think to destroy the abstraction for the sake of the specific is, in this case, an error. Once we come to that realization, it doesn't get quite as confusing as sometimes we tend to treat it.

In my play I was dealing with a young man who would have, I feel, been a compelling object of conflict as a young American of his class of whatever racial background, with the exception of the incident at the end of the play, and with the exception, of course, of character depth, because a Negro character is a reality; there is no such thing as saying that a Negro could be a white person if you just changed the lines or something like this. This is a very arbitrary and superficial approach to Negro character.

But I am taking a long way around to try to answer your question. There really is no profound problem. I started to write about this family as I knew them in the context of those realities which I remembered as being true for this particular given set of people; and, at one point, it was just inevitable that a problem of some magnitude which was racial would intrude itself, because this is one of the realities of Negro life in America. But it was just as inevitable that for a large part of the play, they would be excluded. Because the duality of consciousness is so complete that it is perfectly true to say that Negroes do not sit around 24 hours a day, thinking, "I am a Negro." (LAUGHTER) They really don't. I don't. I don't think he does or anybody else. And, on the other hand, if you say the reverse, that is almost true. And this is part of the complexity that I think you're talking about, isn't it?

BALDWIN: Yes, I agree completely. I think we are bound to get to this, because white men in this country and American Negroes in this country are really the same people. I only discovered this in Europe; perhaps it was always very obvious, but it never occurred to me before. The only people in the world who understand the American white man are American Negroes — (LAUGHTER) — nobody else.

HENTOFF: Langston Hughes, you have a large continuing body of work, and I wondered if you had felt in the course of your long development as a writer, a change in your feeling of this duality as the conditions around you changed, as the struggle for equality became more militant, and the status, to some extent, of the "Negro writer" began to change.

In other words, to what extent did the society around you change the kind of tension under which you wrote?

HUGHES: I must say that I don't notice any changes as yet. (LAUGHTER)

I happen to be a writer who travels a great deal because I read my poems in public and almost every year I travel over most of the country, south and north. I do, of course, see appreciable changes in some areas of race relations and I trust that my recent work reflects that to some extent, but by and large, it seems to me not really very different from when I was a child. There are still a great many places where you can't get a hamburger or a cup of coffee, or you can't sit on a bench in a railroad station, something of this sort — and not just in the South. Those problems exist in Washington, on the West Coast, and in Maine, you know.

I am, of course, as everyone knows, primarily a — I guess you might even say a propaganda writer; my main material is the race problem — and I have found it most exciting and interesting and intriguing to deal with it in writing, and I haven't found the problem of being a Negro in any sense a hindrance to putting words on paper. It may be a hindrance sometimes to selling them; the material that one uses, the fact that one uses, or that I use, problem material, or material that is often likely to excite discussion or disagreement, in some cases prevents its quick sale. I mean, no doubt it's much easier to sell a story like Frank Yerby writes without the race problem in it, or, yes, like Willard Motley, who also happens to be Negro, but writes without emphasizing the sharpness of our American race problem. Those writers are much more commercial than I or, I think, Miss Hansberry, or James Baldwin, who to me seems one of the most racial of our writers, in spite of his analysis of himself as otherwise on occasion.

BALDWIN: Later for you. (LAUGHTER)

KAZIN: Emil Capouya, from what you've observed in publishing as a whole, do you think that Langston Hughes' point has validity, that the degree of sharpness in which the racial problem is written about, is a deterrent to sales, let's say, in the book field? I wonder if there isn't a distinction between magazine writing and book writing here.

CAPOUYA: No, I think not. From an editor's point of view, somebody who's professionally interested in buying or selling literary material, an artist and a writer are two different people.

First of all, he's an artist, and as such his claims are absolute. But he's also a commodity, and as a commodity he has no rights at all. He just has a market value.

So to come directly to your question: Do I think that the material that a Negro writer may find readiest to hand is questionable from a market point of view? I'd say that each writer is an individual case.

Mr. Hughes suggested that it's been a stumbling block on his road to riches, but that wouldn't be the case, obviously, for Mr. Baldwin whose business as a novelist is largely with that material. And Miss Hansberry has had a great success, I think partly because of what that great public that went to see that play thought of as exotic material.

HUGHES: May I say that from long experience with publishers, and many of them — I have about six now — it has been my feeling that if a publisher has one Negro writer on his list or two at the most, he is not very likely to take another if the Negro writer is dealing in Negro themes? And it's not prejudice, it's simply — "Well, we have a book, a Chinese novel on our list. We don't want any more Chinese novels."

And the same thing is true in theater. Once in a blue moon, there's a hit like *Raisin in the Sun,* but the Broadway producers will tell you quite frankly, "No more Negro plays. They're not commercial, we can't sell them. People won't go to the box office."

So if you want to make money out of writing, being a Negro writer, I mean quickly and easily, I would say become a Willard Motley, become a Frank Yerby.

CAPOUYA: I don't think that's the whole truth in relation to the way in which the question was originally posed. Suppose there were two plays about the Jewish East Side —

HUGHES: Yes, it's not a matter really of racial prejudice; it's a matter of the economy we're dealing in.

MISS HANSBERRY: Well, I wouldn't be so quick to decide whether it is or isn't prejudice. There are so many different ways of saying the same thing. It would be more than wishful thinking to me to exclude prejudice regarding Negroes in any area of life. I just don't think that's realistic.

It's prejudice when you can't get an apartment; it's probably prejudice when a skilful writer cannot publish because of some arbitrarily decided notion of what is or is not, as they tell me all the time, parochial material, of narrow interest, and so forth.

In a culture that has any pretensions toward sophistication or interest in human beings, there shouldn't be any designations of kinds of material. A good book should find a publisher.

HUGHES: Since the problem of the writer as a commodity has been brought up, I think it is by and large true to say that for the Negro writer to make a living is doubly hard due to the prejudice that Miss Hansberry has spoken about in other areas related to writing.

For example, I told you that I'm a lecturer and I read my poems. I have been with two or three of the top agencies. Those agencies cannot, as a rule, book me at women's clubs. Women's clubs have teas; they do not wish to mingle socially with their speaker, apparently, and they do not wish to invite their speaker's friends in whatever town he may be speaking on the program, because it's followed by a social event. Therefore, it's a rare occasion when I read my poems to a women's club.

If you want a job in the publishing industry, try and get it. How many editors of color can anyone name on any of our New York publishing houses? You may find an occasional girl secretary at the switchboard or a typist or a stockroom boy, but for the writer himself to get some sort of work related to his actual writing in publishing is well-nigh impossible, I think.

Until very recently, in the last few years, Negroes did not write for Hollywood. Nothing was really sold to Hollywood. That's sort of a new development. I have been writing for 30 years and I've had one Hollywood job in 30 years. Prejudice doesn't keep a writer from writing; if you're colored, you can write all you want to, but you just try and sell it, that's all.

KAZIN: May I go back a moment to the point that Mr. Baldwin began with, this alleged conflict between the social and the artistic in American life?

You know, words like social and artistic are easy to use, and I'm sure that if I had to go through the daily humiliations that certain of my friends go through, I would feel this way.

But let me for a moment, put it on a purely theoretical plane, where art may be discussed. America itself has always been a social question. All that's good in American writing, American art, comes out of the profound confrontation of social facts. It was true of *Moby Dick,* of *Leaves of Grass.* It comes out of what I consider to be the driving force behind all things, which is human hunger, human desire. Only it's a question, of course, not of how much you desire or how bad you feel, but how, artistically, you can realize your desire.

We have to consider two things. One is the current fashion to believe that art is somehow created apart

from society, on the basis of purely individual will, as
opposed to the marvelous books published in this country
between, I would say, 1911 and 1934 or 35, many of
which, like Faulkner's and Steinbeck's, Mr. Hughes' and
other such books, are based on very real and agonizing
social problems. And I must say that in this centenary
year of the Civil War, it's hard to forget that the Negro
is the central issue in American history, has been the
central issue all along, has been the real crux of our
history and our aspirations as a people, and that, therefore, the question that comes up is always how deeply,
how profoundly, how accurately do we recognize this
social kind of drive in our literature right now?

And one thing that's happening right now in middle
class writing everywhere is what's happening to Negroes
too: people don't have as many beefs as they think they
have; they often have no real beefs; they are very often
led by purely arbitrary problems, and consequently, a
good deal of the tremendous whiplash of hunger, hunger
in the widest sense, the deepest sense, has been forgotten
here.

I think — to put it very bluntly — that in America
there cannot be any conflict between the so-called social
and artistic impulse; that one must recognize that what
we call art is the most profound realization of some social
tendency, and that wherever you don't have this social
awareness, social intelligence, then, it seems to me, you
don't have art either.

In other words, the Negro has been not merely a
writer, he's also been a character, and he's been one of
the most profound characters in American literature. I
don't mean Uncle Tom, either. I mean a character from
Faulkner, a character from many, even, pre-Civil War,
novelists, who were always aware of the Negro as a
force, a human being, as a problem, as a challenge, as
a lover, as many things. And one must not forget that
this problem goes to the very essence of our life of civilization.

And that's why I'm so troubled when Mr. Baldwin, for reasons which I can well imagine, but which I want, for once, to pretend I don't understand — opens by bringing up this whole question of the conflict between the social and the artistic.

I think that art is never created when it is too aware of this kind of conflict. I also don't believe in conflicts that are realized. Once there is a conflict, the thing to do is by-pass it and go on to a third force, as such.

I'm thinking, for example, of Mr. Baldwin's *Notes of a Native Son,* which for me, in many ways, is the most brilliant of Negro books, even though it's a collection of essays, of modern American writing. And I've been struck, in rereading it, by the power, the brilliance and the vividness of it.

HUGHES: You know what I would say about it? I would say it's the *Uncle Tom's Cabin* of today. (LAUGHTER)

KAZIN: Well, I happen to like this *Uncle Tom's Cabin.* I think it's a masterpiece.

And the reason it's a masterpiece is because the broken glass of the '43 Harlem riot, the miseries of personal friends — all these things have been captured and realized as a piece of art. And the minute one tries to break away from this, tries to get away from this enormous passion, then one is lost.

The other thing is that one must recognize that art is a word that people use, but the ability to create is something which is utterly God-given, accidental, and capricious. And I think, for example, to speak of something I know rather intimately, when the Jewish immigrants, from whom I come, arrived in this country 50, 60 years ago, there was a whole hoard of sweatshop poets and they were miserable people. They worked 18, 19 hours a day; they lived horrible lives. None of this poetry that I have seen, in English, in Hebrew, or in Yiddish, is any good at all. And then suddenly in the last 15 years, we've had a group of writers, like Saul

Bellow and Norman Mailer and Bernard Malamud and others, who, with enormous surprise to themselves, I think, have suddenly created 5 or 6 really good books, which are as fresh as anything can be.

Now, one reason they've done this is that they've come to recognize their fate as being universal in some sense, and not merely accidental or parochial. I don't mean that they shouldn't write about parochial things, on the contrary, but they've come to recognize the universal in this.

And I ask myself, what is the difference between those lovable, dear people 60 years ago, with their awful sweatshop poetry, and a writer who to my mind is as first-class as Saul Bellow in one or two short things?

I can only say it's a question of the welding together at a certain moment of all these impulses, without for a moment forgetting that intelligence and social passion come into play here. And one mustn't ever try to divide the two. Otherwise, it becomes a problem in the economic history of the writer; it becomes a problem in the social history of the writer; it does not become a problem of art, as such, which is something very different.

BALDWIN: There isn't any conflict between what you said and what I mean. I should clarify my terms some more.

In that particular book review, I was using the conflict between social and artistic responsibility in a very limited and specific way. I know that art comes out of something much deeper than anything that can be named. I know it is always and must be social, because what are you investigating except man and the ways in which he lives, and the ways in which he tries to remake his world, and the ways in which he sometimes fails and sometimes succeeds?

Perhaps I was using the wrong word there; perhaps I should have said propagandistic. Because I don't think there's any point really in blinking this fact and I don't think it can ever be used to defend oneself or excuse oneself for failure, which after all has to be personal and private failure.

Now, there's no point in pretending that being a Negro writer in this country doesn't present certain particular hazards which you would not have if you were white. It is perfectly true, as Langston says, that anybody with his comparable reputation and body of work, who was white, would have much more money than Langston does. This is a fact. But the Negro writer is not as interesting a subject to me as the Negro in this country in the minds of other people — the Negro character, as you put it — and the role that he's always played in the American subconscious, which has never really been dealt with. It has always been there, almost like a corpse which no one knows what to do with, floating in the waters of the national life. And really everything in America can almost be defined by the presence of the Negro in it, including the American personality.

To deal with this, I think, is the real challenge one faces. Somehow actually to unify this country — because it never has been united — and to make a wedding for the first time really, between blacks and whites. Because, this is really the history of a very long love affair, and it's this, much more than anything else which Americans are afraid to look at and don't want to believe.

KAZIN: To use a cryptic phrase, the presence of the Negro in America, in the whole imaginative and moral history of this country, is what I call the central fact.

I've been reading Civil War history for the last few months for an article I'm doing, and I'm struck again and again by the enormous effort so many people made in the '30's and '40's of the last century in the North to overlook the Negroes, to make sure that their little Unitarian, Abolitionist hopes would get rid of him. But again and again the fact came up, it could not be bypassed, and it couldn't be bypassed any more by the

Abolitionists who looked the other way, than it could be bypassed by the Southern slavemasters. And now, in the midst of this agonizing struggle going on in the South, which the whole world is watching, the fact remains, because of the very nature of American democracy, that never in history has a whole body of former slaves been made the issue of human and civic equality on such a large scale as in this country.

The love affair, which I would say is more a mutual and fascinated awareness of each other, is itself the very incidence of the agony and passion of the Negro's presence in American life. And this is why, when you recognize the social factor, as Faulkner does in his best work — and I'm not thinking here of Joe Christmas — I'm thinking here of the total context he creates — then you recognize the depth of emotion, the depth of commitment out of which art can come.

Now, the economic problem is something else. It is disgusting that a lecturer should have to be banned from a women's tea club because he might have to have tea with them.

But think what a marvelous story this makes, about America: people who think they would like to hear the lecturer are afraid to have the tea. Note the slightly comic element, not in the sense of being amiable, but in revealing human paradox and hypocrisy.

When I was a professor at a New England college some years ago, there were two Negro boys in the college, a testimony to its Abolitionist background. And, of course, these boys were miserable and about as lonely as a spar of wood on a Cape Cod beach. But the fact remains that out of this kind of experience would come to an artist, white or Negro, a sense of the extraordinary comedy of social hopes and moral would-be feelings of this country, too — which is, I submit, as close to the life of art as the suffering and anxiety of an individual writer who happens to be a Negro here. And this is why I hope that we will not only remember, as we all must, what is happening to each of us who is a Negro down South, but also of the enormous presence of the Negro as a fact in the American imagination, which again and again has created something which is absolutely inextricable — it cannot be lost, cannot be forgotten, cannot be bypassed, in our minds for a moment.

HUGHES: Speaking of the celebration of the centennial of the Civil War, I have just written yesterday columns for *The Chicago Defender,* for which I write, using my Simple character as a kind of social protest mouthpiece, and I'd like to read you a section because it involves the very thing that you're talking about.

Simple is in the barbershop and this is what he says:

"I sit in that barber chair, thinking about how God must love poor folks because he made so many of them in my image. (LAUGHTER.)

"You know, as long as I've been poor, I'm not used to it. My papa were poor before me and my grandpa were poorer that that, being a slave which did not even own hisself. So, I was settin in that barberchair thinking, one day the time might come when I will own Old Master's grandson, since him nor none of his white relations won't let me get hold a nothing else."

"What on earth are you talking about," I asked, "reinstating slavery? Are you out of your mind?"

"I was sort of dozin and dreamin whilst he cut my hair," said Simple, "and in snoozin I kept thinkin about how much I been hearin about this here centennial of the Civil War and stuff the white folks has been tellin — intendin to celebrate in honor of the North and South. And they're going to be on parades and meetins and battles and things like they were 100 years ago. One way of makin people remember what that Civil War were all about might be to bring back slavery for a month or two, only this time, reverse it. Make the white folks the slaves and me the master.

"I would like to own some of them white Simples on my grandma's side, which were the ones, I understand, that gave me my name. Oh, I would like to own a few white folks just once." (LAUGHTER) "Maybe I could work out of them some of the money that they owe my great-grandfolks and never did pay. Else make up for these low wages which I'm gettin right now.

"I would like to own me some rich white slaves, not used to workin like me for hardly enough to pay income tax when April, let alone Harlem rent and balancing your budget."

"Dream on," I said.

"From dawn to long after dark, I would find something for them white folks to do," said Simple, "if I owned them, and come the end of the week, not pay them a cent. That would be a real good way, I figure, to celebrate the centennial. Make it real, not just play-actin, but bring slavery back to its own doorstep. One hundred years, it is time to turn the tables.

"But don't you know, since I was dreamin about all this, the barber cut my hair too short?"

"It looks all right to me," I said, "In fact, I would say, with you, the less hair the better."

"I might have bad hair," said Simple, "But I've got a good-shaped head." (LAUGHTER)

Well now, I very often try to use social material in a humorous form and most of my writing from the very beginning has been aimed largely at a Negro reading public, because when I began to write I had no thought of achieving a wide public. My early work was always published in *The Crisis* of the NAACP, and then in *The Opportunity* of the Urban League, and then the Negro papers like the *Washington Sentinel* and the *Baltimore American,* and so on. And I contend that since these things, which are Negro, largely for Negro readers, have in subsequent years achieved world-wide publication — my work has come out in South America, Japan, and all over Europe — that a regional Negro character like Simple, a character intended for the people who belong to his own race, if written about warmly enough, humanly enough, can achieve universality.

In fact, I think my Simple character has achieved universality with the very kind of thing that he talks about here in the barber chair, because all around the world poor people have economic problems, all around the world, in almost every country, there is some sort of racial problem. In Japan it's — what do they call them? — the Ainu; in India, it's the Untouchables; in France, it's the *sales Algériens*.

These problems are not limited just to America. But they impose no limitation on the writer one way or another.

Norman Mailer was mentioned — I didn't know he was a Jewish writer until right now — he achieved a universality, in spite of his Jewish background.

And I don't see, as Jimmy Baldwin sometimes seems to imply, any limitations, in artistic terms, in being a Negro. I see none whatsoever. It seems to me that any Negro can write about anything he chooses, even the most narrow problems: if he can write about it forcefully and honestly and truly, it is very possible that that bit of writing will be read and understood, in Iceland or Uruguay.

KAZIN: I agree entirely, Mr. Hughes. I was thinking about the difference between two of Richard Wright's books, one of which moved me enormously when I was younger than I am now, *Native Son*, the other, *The Outsider*, which I didn't like at all. I agree with you entirely about the need to be parochial, the need to write out of one's milieu and to one's milieu; in fact, Wright's *The Outsider* is my text to prove it.

When I read about this Negro on a train meeting this hunchback, who made common cause with him because they were both symbols of the outsider, I thought this was weak artistically; I felt it was, as the French say, *voulu*, it was willed, it was not real. What seemed to me to be absolutely legitimate, however, were the profoundly touching scenes in which Bigger was involved in *Native Son,* which still is a very powerful and enormously moving book.

We Americans are very symbolic to ourselves as well as to other people. And very often we think of ourselves as being in the forefront of the world. (I think we still are. I still think we're more revolutionary than any other country in the world, at least implicitly, in terms of the kind of society we're trying to build.)

But the point I'm getting at is that the Negro tends very often today to think of himself as being the symbol of man in the outside world, because of the enormous fact of the race problem in all countries of the world, because of the enormous suffering and wars going on right now. The Negro middle-class writer in America, may, if he is in Paris, as Wright was, think of himself as being the symbol rather than the fact. And my point is that only when the Negro thinks of himself as a fact can art begin. The minute he thinks of himself as a symbol, then theory creeps in and the whole problem is dis-social, dis-artistic.

When you're writing out of the actual broken glass of the actual confused heats of that race riot in '43 in the Harlem streets, when Jimmy took his father to the grave, then you have the beginning of what you don't understand too well.

There is a certain law for art: not to know as you're writing what everything means. It's being impressed with the fact, not with the significance of the fact. Too often one tends, because of the enormous centrality of the Negro position today in world experience, to say, "Well, we all know what that means," but we don't. It all goes back to one house, one street, one uncle or grandmother, or whatever.

MISS HANSBERRY: I don't think that there should be any overextended attention to this question of what is or what isn't universal.

I think that Simple, for instance, is as kin to the

Shakespearean wise fool as any other character in literature I've ever heard of, but we don't notice the Englishness of a Shakespearean fool while we're being entertained and educated by his wisdom; the experience just happens. It happens because people have rent problems everywhere in the world and because men are oppressed everywhere in the world. The point of contact is innate to the piece to the extent that it is true, to the extent that it is art, which is what I think that you were saying.

I have been distressed personally, in connection with something that Mr. Kazin was saying, having to do with the traditional treatment of Negro characters in American literature — let's speak now of non-Negro writers. I was perplexed to find, when I addressed myself to that question in two popular essays, that nobody seemed to know what on earth I was talking about — which, of course, could be a matter of delivery. On one occasion I tried to discuss the character, Walter Lee, the young man in my play, in terms of why, as you said a moment ago, in the so-called white mind, he was still an expression of exoticism, no matter how he had been created. Many people, apparently, recognized his humanity, but he was still exotic to them.

In my opinion, since man is so complex and since I disagree with most of the despairing crowd, if you're going to get ridiculous and talk about man being basically anything, you may as well say he's probably basically good. If that is true, then it is also true that man is trying to accommodate his own guilt always, all of us.

And it seems to me that one of the things that has been done in the American mentality is to create this escape valve of the exotic Negro, wherein it is possible to exalt abandon on all levels, and to imagine that while I am dealing with the perplexities of the universe, look over there, coming down from the trees — (LAUGHTER) — is a Negro who knows none of this, and wouldn't it be marvelous if I could be my naked brutal, savage self again?

This permeates our literature in every variation: I don't believe that Negro characters as created thus far have overcome that problem. I don't even believe that the Negro artist has overcome it, because we have been affected by it.

For example, the Emperor Jones is not a man in conflict with the world. He is an arch-symbol that never existed on land, sea, or under it; and to the extent that we recognize something about him, we recognize something symbolized in our own minds. I think this would also be true of Porgy.

The discussion of the Negro character has been so primitive in the past, we've been so busy talking about who's a stereotype and who isn't, we have never talked about it as art. I maintain that the problem is that these characters as they've appeared in literature have never gained full human stature because the writers who have created them haven't thought about them as men in the first place. It isn't a matter of just wanting to change how they speak. Everytime you say something about *Porgy and Bess,* somebody says, "Well, you know, Negroes did speak dialect 40 years ago." Heavens, they still do. That is not the argument; the argument is that Porgy is not a man.

KAZIN: No, he isn't. I think that American literature written by white people is probably 99.9 per cent full of these stereotypes and that lately we have been treated to the worst stereotype of all, which is what Norman Mailer calls the "White Negro," namely, the noble savage brought back as an example to the bourgeois white American.

BALDWIN: I have some objections to Faulkner's Negro characters. I'll try to tell you what they are. I think the principal one is that not only is there something left out, there is something left out that should be there. Even in the great portrait of Joe Christmas — the only way is to put it as bluntly as possible, then we can go back and modify it — there is something about him which rubs me the wrong way, and it's not his situation and it isn't his dialect, it isn't any of these things at all. What it is is that he's also a kind of apology for an injustice which is really still not being dealt with.

Now Faulkner is a very good example of what I mean. The Southern writers who have written about Negroes and have written about them well have all written about them in more or less the same way, essentially out of a feeling of guilt. What is most mysterious is that it is a guilt to which they cling. It's a guilt without which their identities would be threatened. What is so fascinating about this whole Negro-white relationship in America, is what it means in the American personality to have a Negro around. That is why he's always the noble savage in no matter what guise, from Eisenhower to Norman Mailer, nobody can give this up. Everybody wants to have this sort of walking symbol around to protect something in themselves which they do not want to examine.

But what one deals with in the world every day, really, isn't the world's malice or even the world's indifference, it's the world's ignorance. And it's not ignorance of the Negro or the fact of Negro life as such. It's an ignorance of a certain level of life which no one has ever respected or it's never been real in America. You can almost say — you can say, in fact — that one of the reasons that the Negro is at the bottom of the social heap in America, is because it's the only way everyone in America will know where the bottom is. (LAUGHTER)

KAZIN: Exactly, as you put it, marvelously, to show us where the bottom is, where everything that is fundamental is in our country. But at the bottom, there are people who, understandably because they've been at the bottom so long, will be seen by an imaginative writer like Faulkner in a certain way.

Now, would you want Faulkner to write about the Negro only, so to speak, as he *should* be in our minds, if he were given a chance, or do you want him out of all these hundreds of years of Southern bondage and Southern slaveowning and Southern prejudice to release that powerful talent and throw it away?

Let me put this in a personal way, if I may — I too come from people who are not altogether unused to prejudice. Now, only 15 years ago a million and a half Jewish children were put into bonfires by the Nazis just because they were Jewish children. It's a terrible fact, part of the incredible oppression of the second World War. Nevertheless, if I read Shakespeare's *Merchant of Venice,* with its venomous, unbearable portrait of Shylock, though I think it's false, I have to admit it's a great artistic creation. And it seems to me that over the years, one thing that's happened to me as a writer in America, is that I've learned to say that Shylock is a great character and not worry about him so much.

Don't misunderstand me, though. I'm not trying to sermonize on this question. All I'm saying here is that we do have a handful of books that seem to be written out of the bottom, and one musn't presume too much here too, for this reason: Joe Christmas is not a Negro. No one knows what or who he is. People think he's a Negro, and the point in that great novel — *Light in August* is a very great book, an extraordinary book — is that because people do not know him, but merely see in him what they think he is, not what he really is (he could be anything) — they do everything to him right up to the end. They murder him, they castrate him, and he becomes the dead Christ on the American cross. Again and again, it's made clear, that the fact of Negro suffering has created this figure.

On the other hand, when Faulkner writes a letter to *The New York Times* about segregation in the South, he writes like a damn fool, he writes like any typical, vulgar Mississippian. When he writes a novel which has a Negro character in it, he's a great artist.

HUGHES: Oh, certainly, he's an amazingly good

writer. However, it seems to me that he doesn't really and fully understand even the Southern Negro with whom he's lived all his life. Did you see *Requiem for a Nun,* last season?

KAZIN: Yes. It was terrible. I hated *Requiem for a Nun,* both as a book and as a play.

HUGHES: In that play he has this Negro woman who is going to her death for having committed some sort of murder, I believe, which she felt was justified, and the lawyer or the judge is talking to her, and she says she doesn't mind dying, in essence, because she is going to Heaven. And this Southern white lawyer, judge, or whatever he is, says, "What would a woman like you do in Heaven?" And she says, "Ah kin work." Now, that is the most false line in literature regarding the Negro, because no Negro in God's world ever thought of Heaven as a place to work. He just doesn't understand the Negro mind, that's all.

KAZIN: But as a writer, and a very good writer, do you think it's necessary to understand something in order to create a good character? Is understanding, in the deepest human, civic sense, the brotherly sense, is this really necessary for artistic creation?

HUGHES: To create a believable character, you certainly have to have a certain amount of understanding. And this woman in *Requiem* became so unreal to me.

KAZIN: Yes, I agree with you about that case, but let's consider Dilsey. She was also a Southern Negro, and a character who would cause me the deepest pain and chagrin if I were a Negro; nevertheless, I believe she is a great creation.

HUGHES: Yes, I don't doubt that.

KAZIN: Well, you can't understand Negroes on one page and forget them on another. Because understanding is always the same. It's typical Faulkner, who reveals his limitations in non-artistic areas. But as a writer, once in a while, something is created which comes out of the deepest, most unconscious sense of love.

Let me give you an instance: you may remember that the fourth part of *The Sound and the Fury* opens with Dilsey coming out on the porch. She is portrayed in a typical hand-me-down costume of a woman who has worked for 50 years for this rotting family, the Compsons. The costume itself is demeaning, but the description of Dilsey, everything about her, is of such an extraordinary artistic beauty and intensity that I can never read it without being moved to tears. The thing has been made flesh, and she is there, we know her. This is something very different, I submit, from 101 moralizings that you might get from well-meaning Northern "liberals."

All I'm saying is that on this page — and on many pages of that book — he really created a human being, and even when he sees her without understanding in his mind, there was tremendous understanding in his heart.

HUGHES: Yes, and I think another fine Southern white writer, Carson McCullers, is also successful in creating character.

MISS HANSBERRY: I think, Mr. Kazin, that you may be imposing on my earlier remarks a lack of dimension that wasn't there. What I was trying to say is exactly the opposite of what you emphasized. I am not concerned with doing away with the mere traditional paraphernalia of the inexpressive, crude Negro character. That is not the point. I myself, very arbitrarily, after deliberate thought, chose to write about the Negro working class, although I come from the middle class. Eventually, I think more of our writers are going to begin to deal with the Negro middle class, which most white people don't know exists.

But we're not trying to escape from some image of truth. When you spoke a moment ago, you seemed to suggest we would be satisfied if the image were more glossy, more dressed-up. That is not the point. When language is handled truly, and Negro speech used with fidelity — which doesn't have to do with the dropping of g's and misplacing of verbs — when the essence of character is as true and as complicated as — as character should be, whatever character you're dealing with, only then ought we to be satisfied.

There is a comedy line in my play, where the young daughter says to one of her suitors, "You think this about women because this is what you got from all the novels that men have written." Obviously, novelists have created some memorable women characters. But I am altogether certain that in regard to the inner truths of character, the woman character will always partially elude the male writer. Of course, women, like Negroes, I'm afraid, accept many images of themselves that come from literature, and start to act those roles, but there are other truths, which can be found only by studying people in depth.

You mentioned Carson McCullers. There's a scene in *Member of the Wedding,* when the young Negro nephew of Bernice is being chased by a lynch mob, and she takes the young white boy whom she has nursed all his life — he's about to die, I think, because of some constitutional weakness — and this woman's preoccupation is with that child. I happen to think that it was a lovely play and I believe Bernice's character, but we are now talking about these extra nuances, and my point is that the intimacy of knowledge with the Negro may have of white Americans does not exist in the reverse.

KAZIN: That's absolutely true.

MISS HANSBERRY: William Faulkner has never in his life sat in on a discussion in a Negro home where there were all Negroes. It is physically impossible. He has never heard the nuances of hatred, of total contempt from his most devoted servant and his most beloved friend, although she means every word when she's talking to him, and will tell him profoundly intimate things. But he has never heard the truth of it. For you, this is a fulfilling image, because you haven't either. I can understand that. Obviously Faulkner is a monumental talent, but there are other dimensions of that character, and as I would create her, or Jim, or Langston, there would be a world of difference, and it's this we're trying to get to. I *want* white writers to begin to create Negro characters. We need it desperately.

BALDWIN: Lorraine's point is very important. We have to look more carefully at the characters created by Faulkner, or by Carson McCullers. Lorraine mentioned that absolutely incredible moment when this woman's nephew is being chased by a lynch mob, and she's worried about this little boy. That scene doesn't reveal anything about the truth of Negro life, but a great deal about the state of mind of the white Southern woman who wrote it.

Regardless of Faulkner's talent, the thing I will not settle for is that this image is maintained. Southerners have an illusion and they cling to it desperately; in fact, the whole American Republic does. These characters come out of a compulsion. Dilsey is Faulkner's proof that the Negro — who, as Langston points out, has been worked and worked and worked and for nothing, who has been lynched and burned and stolen from for generations — has forgiven him. The reason the walls in the South cannot come down, the reason that the panic is too great for the walls to come down, is because when they do, the truth will come out. And it's perfectly true, as Lorraine says, you can't know what I'm talking about, if you haven't been in a home with all Negroes together, if you haven't listened to Dilsey at home — who might be my mother — and heard what she says about the people she works for — and what is more important than that, not only what she says, but what she knows. And she knows much more about them than they will ever know about her, and there's a very good reason for this.

Faulkner has never sat in a Negro kitchen while the Negroes were talking about him, but we have been sitting around for generations, in kitchens and everywhere else, while everybody talks about us, and this creates a very great difference. It also creates — now speaking specifically for the Negro writer — a very great advantage. While I was living abroad in France, somebody said something — it's something, I guess, the French say all the time — but this day it was said to me and it rang a bell. He said, "If you want to know what's happening in the house, ask the maid." And it occurred to me that in this extraordinary house, I'm the maid. (LAUGHTER)

MISS HANSBERRY: Which is a different relationship, because the employer doesn't go to the maid's house. You see, people get this confused. They think that the alienation is equal on both sides. It isn't. We have been washing everybody's underwear for 300 years. We know when you're not clean. (LAUGHTER)

KAZIN: I accept everything you say, Miss Hansberry, but I wonder if you would allow me to try to persuade you that it's still slightly irrelevant to the point I was making.

MISS HANSBERRY: Oh, then I'm sorry.

KAZIN: No, no; as I was irrelevant to your point, you're being irrelevant to mine. This is the way people learn to talk to each other.

My point is this: I don't for a moment mean to say that the truth about Negro life has been accomplished, to use the Biblical phrase, forever. I'm talking about what has actually been done as art.

This is an artistic question, it's not a social question. I know that Negroes have been maids, they have been the drawers of water and the hewers of wood. They have been the slaves and slaves do all the work.

But my point is this: it's something Edward Hopper, the painter, once said, which has stuck in my mind: "Thought is endless, but the picture exists in space and time."

Every Negro walking the streets, every American, is full of the past, the present and the future. No book, either his book or a white man's book, can satisfy him about the truth. Because the truth is not only about what he has and what he is, but what he wants to become, what he wants America to become. Therefore, there is no book that exists right now that in the deepest sense can be satisfying to him.

But a book does exist in space and time. Those distortions of Shylock, or of Dilsey, or of anyone else, horrible as they are to our conscience, nevertheless exist as such. Dostoyevski, Tolstoy, Melville, all the great novelists, have written the most frightfully distorted anti-Negro, anti-Japanese, anti-Semitic, anti-French stereotypes. Do American characters come off much better, in American fiction as a whole? Not always in contemporary American fiction. They are portrayed uniformly as lechers, sadists, masturbators, idiots, bourgeois decadents and the rest. This is a society that is full of self-disgust. It doesn't know what it wants or what it believes, and it's constantly getting rid of its own guilt about its own unsatisfied wantings in that way.

My point is that a book exists in itself, as such, and perhaps — it's hard for a writer to admit — perhaps, all of us who write books are not so busy mirroring life, as we always think we are, as creating life.

For example, Tolstoy created a great book like *War and Peace* and then looked about him and found out something about the actual conditions of serfdom and contemporary Russia; he discovered, what his wife had told him beforehand, that the two things — the thing he had created and the world around him — had nothing to do with each other in any immediate sense.

This is a terrible paradox. But the fact remains that there are no people anywhere like the people in our books or anybody else's book.

Simple is delicious and wise and right because he is a product of Mr. Hughes' imagination. Many people have gone into making him up. He is no one else, he is Simple. This is true of any true character.

It's even true of a good autobiography like Jimmy Baldwin's *Notes of a Native Son,* where we find that the author himself becomes his own myth, as Thoreau said about himself in *Walden.*

I am not trying to say that Mr. Faulkner is the last word on Negroes in America. God forbid. What I am saying is that something was created, something was not just being talked about, hopeful and wishful, all the time. Something that is true, I think, as such.

BALDWIN: We are talking somewhat at cross purposes, because I cannot disagree with what you say.

KAZIN: But there isn't any argument. We are reflecting on a problem which has many facets. I don't disagree with you about this thing at all. How can I? What is there to disagree about? Do you think I would say that Dilsey is the truth about Negroes in America? That would be a horrible untruth.

BALDWIN: All right, I accept the proposition that perhaps we are not so much reflecting life as trying to create it — but let's talk now not about books but about this country.

I'm talking now about the role of the Negro, and what seems to me to be at stake is that somehow the Negro contains a key to something about America which no one has yet found out about — which no one has yet faced. Contains maybe the key to life. I don't know; I don't want to talk about it in such mythical terms.

My point is that there is a tremendous resistance on the part of the entire public to know whatever it is, to deal with whatever this image means to them.

HENTOFF: I wonder how many doors that key unlocks.

Langston Hughes has mentioned the urge to whiteness among some Negro writers. This leads, of course, to assimilationist novels, but I wonder if it doesn't also lead, without complete realization on the part of some Negro writers, politicians, and others, to a desire for equality within the white value-structure. Has there been enough questioning of this within Negro writing?

BALDWIN: I feel that there's been far too little.

HENTOFF: In other words, equal for what?

BALDWIN: Equal for what, yes. You know, there's always been a very great question in my mind of why in the world — after all I'm living in this society and I've had a good look at it — what makes you think I want to be accepted?

MISS HANSBERRY: Into this.

BALDWIN: Into this.

MISS HANSBERRY: Maybe something else.

BALDWIN: It's not a matter of acceptance or tolerance. We've got to sit down and rebuild this house.

MISS HANSBERRY: Yes, quickly.

BALDWIN: Very quickly, and we have to do it together. This is to you, Alfred, speaking now, just as a writer. You know, in order to be a writer you have to demand the impossible, and I know I'm demanding the impossible. It has to be — but I also know it has to be done. You see what I mean?

KAZIN: Yes, I see entirely what you mean, but let's talk about this presence of the Negro in American history for a moment, because when we really get into the question of the white writers' portraits of Negroes we're talking about this larger question. Maybe that way we can come back to the difficulty we had earlier.

This presence of the Negro in American civilization, I said before, is the central fact about our moral history. And the conflict in the American heart, which exists in Negroes as well as among whites, comes out of a constant tension between what this country is ideally supposed to mean and what it actually has been as such. The problem has become more and more catastrophic and dangerous because of the growing world anxiety about possible world annihilation. Suddenly you begin to realize that people who don't treat their fellow-citizens well are, in a sense, building up a bonfire for everyone else in the same way, as is likely to happen in Africa before our generation is over.

At the same time, this very tension in America between the ideal moral purpose and the reality also creates two things. One, it creates the fact that we never know quite what we want, as you yourself admitted before. You said you weren't quite sure you wanted equality to disrupt you. And secondly, it creates the white man's constant bewilderment between what he feels abstractly to be his duty, and the actuality of a society in which human beings were held as slaves, and in which, 25 years later, these people were sitting in Washington as senators.

So you have this enormous comedy of American pretension and American actuality, leaving the white man, who is also here, in a constant bewilderment. But whereas you spoke of guilt, I think it's more a sense of an intellectual paradox. Because in order to justify his own presence in this country, the white American has to understand the Negro's place, but to understand it fully, he has to make a gesture of imagination, morally — even religiously, in the deepest sense of the word; yet very often he is debased by his own culture and kept from making this gesture. But this is what happened again and again. This is what happened with the Civil War.

Let's put it this way: Who in American history among the white writers or white men did make the fullest effort of imagination in your point of view?

It wasn't the Abolitionists; it wasn't Colonel Higginson, leading Negro troops in the Civil War. Who was it? Who would you say it was? I think it's been no one. I think it's a fight which has constantly been in process, constantly going on. But nowhere, in no particular point in space and time can you say this has been understood fully and deeply.

HUGHES: To go back to Jimmy Baldwin's point, at

the first Negro Writer's Conference, a year and a half ago, and published in *The American Negro Writer and His Roots,* is a speech by Julian Mayfield, one of our better young Negro novelists. Speaking of the examination of American values by American Negro writers, this is what he says:

"This new approach is suggested by the Negro mother, who having lost one of her sons in the Korean adventures, was heard to remark, 'I don't care if the Army is integrated, next time I want to know what kind of war my boy is being taken into.'

"In the same sense, the Negro writer is being very gently nudged toward a rather vague thing called the mainstream of American literature. This trend would also seem to be based on common sense. But before plunging into it, he owes it to the future of his art to analyze the contents of the American mainstream, to determine the full significance of his commitment to it.

"He may decide that though the music is sweet, he would rather play in another orchestra; or to place himself in the position of the black convict in *The Defiant Ones,* he may decide that he need not necessarily share the fate of his white companion, who after all proffers the hand of friendship a little late. The Negro writer may conclude that his best salvation lies in escaping the narrow national orbit, artistic, cultural and political, and soaring into the space of more universal experience."

HENTOFF: In this regard I'd like to bring up one further thing before we conclude, concerning the future.

In an otherwise rather strange book, *The Negro Novel in America,* by Boone, he has statistics showing that of 62 Negro novelists writing between 1853 and 1952, 40, or two-thirds, published only one novel, 11 more published only 2, and only 11 have published more than two.

Is this largely due to economic discrimination and the like, or is it due to a self-limitation to a single theme, which could only be expressed once?

HUGHES: My guess would be that it was largely

due to the limitation of thematic material, and secondarily due to the fact of economics, due to the fact that the Negro people themselves, of whom there are now about 20 million in our country, have not one single publishing house.

We discussed a while ago, you remember, the limitation placed upon the number of Negro novels that can be published in a year.

The same thing is true in the theater. Do we have one serious Negro dramatic theater that belongs to us, that is managed by us, that is directed by us? No. The nearest thing we have to it is Karamu Theatre in Cleveland, which is a part of a settlement house. Formerly it was largely Negro attended, but it does such beautiful productions that now more than two-thirds of its personnel is white, because white people come from all over to work in Karamu. They used to do plays by Negro writers almost entirely, about Negro life, but not anymore. The trend is to integrate everything, so that you kill yourself with an integrated cast.

The trend toward integration in some cases, particularly in the folk field, in my opinion, can go too far, in that it is damaging artistically. For example, I narrated a Gospel song program in Chicago, a winter or two ago, with Mahalia Jackson, and do you know that the people who presented the program integrated the Gospel singers? Mahalia listened and gathered her fur coat about her at rehearsal, and went home with the parting shot, "Y'all ain't got the beat."

There is a tendency at the moment, in jazz, to integrate every combo, which is wonderful, sociologically speaking. But very often the white players who may come into a combo, will not have that same beat, let us say, that Jonah Jones has, you know what I mean?

MISS HANSBERRY: Are we just skirting around a larger political question in an effort to avoid it, perhaps? Because, what are we faced with? We are faced with the fact that due to these 300 years of the experience of black people in the Western hemisphere — not only in the United States, though it was least successful in the United States — a possible difference of ultimate cultural attitudes now exists as a reality, so that in May-field's statement that you read just now, there are the tones of Negro nationalism, articulated in a far more sophisticated and pointed way than years ago. The question is openly being raised today among all Negro intellectuals, among all politically-conscious Negroes: — is it necessary to integrate oneself into a burning house? And we can't quite get away from it.

There are real and true things existing in the consciences of Negroes today which have to do with why, on two occasions, the American Negro delegate at the United Nations disassociated herself from her government, when we refused to vote for an Algerian Algeria, when we refused to vote for the end of colonialism. When the most compromised element in the Negro population, from which these people are drawn — I mean no offense personally to that lady, I don't even know who she is, but there is only a certain section of Negro life that is allowed to represent us — when they are moved to disassociate themselves in an international hall, and when 10,000 Negroes will come out to greet Fidel Castro in Harlem and wave at him and cheer him everytime he shows his head, this is an indication of what is going on. This dichotomy is going to become more articulate and we are going to see it more and more in Negro literature.

HUGHES: I would like to say that in Lorraine Hansberry's play the thing that comes through is that, in spite of all these differences and difficulties, *this is our house.* That was their Chicago. This is our country. And I for one am intensely concerned and fascinated, by the things that go on here.

Some people have asked me why Richard Wright didn't come home and why he lived in Europe, and why some of our better Negro artists and writers are living over there. My feeling is that they have a perfect right to live wherever they want to, and to get away from the tensions of the American scene, if they wish. It just happens that it interests me, it doesn't upset me particularly. I like to indulge in these racial arguments and fights and discussions, such as we are having here, about what to do about all this. And I stayed here and I live here because I like it, quite frankly, and I think that we can make out of our country something wonderful and quite beautiful, in which eventually we can integrate Gospel songs and have them sung well.

CAPOUYA: I'd like to raise a question regarding the sit-in movements in the South. Certainly, a Negro ought to be able to eat where everybody else does; since he's a brother of mine, obviously, that's the first step, before I can be free to eat where I want, too.

But a couple of years ago, when the march on Washington was made, the Negro leaders were saying, "After all, you people are fighting for your lives, you're fighting against the Russians. Why don't you admit us to that status of citizenship where we can help you? Why don't you admit us to the community so we can pull our weight?"

Well, that's a lot of nonsense as far as I'm concerned, and if that's what they're out to get, if they want to get atomized at the same time we do, we'll all be holding hands in Christian brotherly love when the bomb falls. Well, that is stupid.

I would be delighted if the Rev. Martin Luther King would think one step ahead of himself in this sense, and not feel that civil rights for Negroes in the South is the be-all and the end-all. It may be a tactical first step, but if it isn't to move to a higher plane, then I'm not interested.

HUGHES: Well, I heard Rev. Martin Luther King say at a meeting not long ago that perhaps it was the Negro's destiny to save America for itself. And another rather distinguished Negro leader disagreed and said,

"Well, first, certainly, we've got to save it for ourselves."

BALDWIN: I'm delighted that we've got around to this very thorny area. It has always seemed to me that one of the great handicaps of this country in its dealings with the world is that it doesn't know anything about the rest of the world, not in the sense that a Frenchman doesn't know anything about China, but in the sense that it has always avoided knowing those things — I'm afraid you have to call them tragic or black or deep or mysterious or inexorable — which are at the very bottom of life.

One of the reasons that Cuba has been such a disaster is because people in America do not know that just down the road Mexicans and Cubans, and a whole lot of other people in a place called South America, are not only starving, which you can tell by statistics, but are living there. And they don't like to be mistreated. And one of the reasons that we don't know this, is our evasion in the world, which is exactly the evasion that we've made in this country for over 100 years, to date it only from the emancipation. Ultimately, it's a moral evasion of oneself, which really menaces — and this cannot be overstated — the very future of this country. That is why there is so little time to save this house; after all, one can always jump, that's not the problem. I don't want to be atomized with you or with anybody, and I don't want anybody else atomized, either.

But the price for American survival is really the most extraordinary and speedy metamorphosis, and I don't know if they're going to make it. But we've got to realize that when people say God, they don't always mean the Protestant God. There are people on the other side of the world, who have been worshipping somebody else for thousands and thousands of years. I do think that anybody who really cares about this must insist on nothing more or less than a moral revolution. Because nothing can be patched up. It's got to be remade.

CAPOUYA: That's so true, but I want to object to

something said before, the notion of the white man's guilty secret, and that the Negro has got to be where he is because we have to know where the bottom of the heap is. That's not true: the Negro is where he is because of the long history of slavery, economic rejection, and so on.

HUGHES: At the moment I have a play which I hope will be on Broadway next season. The play was originally entirely about Negroes — about the Gospel churches. However, with the current trend towards integration, some backers said that they would not put money into an entirely Negro-cast play.

Well, the leading lady in my play, who makes a great deal of money out of selling holy water, worked up to having a chauffeur; in my script it never occurred to me that he should be one color or another. I thought of him as a Negro chauffeur because most Negroes who can afford chauffeurs have Negro chauffeurs, but not all. However, when the demand came for integration of my cast, I said, "Well, always in white plays the chauffers are Negroes; let's make the chauffeur in my play white, which would not be untrue to life." Adam Powell, I believe, has a white or Japanese chauffeur. Jules Bledso, when he was star of "Showboat" had a white chauffeur, and when people asked him why he had a white chauffeur, he said, "So people can tell the chauffeur from myself." (LAUGHTER)

Well, at any rate, it's not too unusual that some colored people do have white chauffeurs and some have white maids, even in Harlem. And so I thought that would be nice and a little novel to Broadway. Let's have a white chauffeur. Do you know that everybody said, "Oh, the American public wouldn't accept that"? So my play is still not integrated.

MISS HANSBERRY: I gather we are close to conclusion, but, Mr. Kazin, I'd like to pick up something that you said, and to try and bring it up to date for myself.

You said, I thought rather beautifully, that the Negro question tends to go to the heart of various missorted American agonies, beginning with slavery itself. I am profoundly concerned that in these 100 years since the Civil War very few of our countrymen have really believed that their Federal Union and the defeat of the slavocracy and the negation of slavery as an institution is an admirable fact of American life. It is possible today to get enormous books that are coming out on the Civil War and go through to the back of them, and not find the word slavery, let alone Negro.

We've been trying very hard in America to pretend that this great conflict didn't even have at its base the only issue that was significant. Person after person will write a book today and insist that slavery was not the issue. They tell you that it was fought for economic reasons, as if that economy were not based on slavery. People spend volumes discussing the battles of the Civil War and which army was crossing the river at five minutes to two and how their swords were hanging, but we have tried to get rid of the slavery issue. Ever since *Gone With the Wind,* it has been an accepted part of our culture to describe the slave system in terms of beautiful ladies in big fat dresses, screaming that their houses have been burned down by the awful Yankees. But when someone asked me to write 90 minutes of television drama on slavery, not a propaganda piece, but, I hope, a serious treatment of family relationships, by a slave-owning family and their slaves, this was considered controversial. This has never been done.

Those millions of Americans who went out only a month or two ago, presumably voted for a Federal president, but our culture does not really respect the fact that if the North had not won, if the Union forces had not triumphed over slavery, this country that we're talking about would exist only in imagination. Americans today are too ashamed and frightened to take a position even on this.

BALDWIN: Yes, this breaks the heart; this is the most sinister thing about it. Not that it happened, not that it's wrong, but that nobody wants to admit that it happened. And until this admission is made, nothing can be done.

KAZIN: How much time do we have?

HENTOFF: Is there anything you want to add?

KAZIN: We should begin the interview.